CHAPTER I
THE COUNTRY

"Norte-Americano," politely suggested a Brazilian to me in the course of a conversation, and I accepted the correction.

"We also are *Americanos*," he continued. After that I was very careful to make the distinction, although in an unguarded moment it would sometimes appear. "*Ingles*" or "*Norte-Americano*," would sometimes be asked, although the most of the Brazilians can spot the "*Yanqui*," as he is called with all due respect. It is said that our former Secretary of State, during his circular tour around South America, was very careful in all his speeches to call himself a North American, and this one little distinction aided in increasing his popularity. It is often the delicate little recognition that pleases these Latin people, who are themselves full of flattery and compliments. It is time for the people of the United States, especially as they are now entering upon an era of commercial conquest, to recognize that these people of the great continent south of us are just as much entitled to the use of that term, of which they are likewise proud, as we ourselves are; that though these people are Brazilians, Argentinians, Chileans, etc., they consider themselves first and foremost as Americans, in order to distinguish themselves from Europeans, Asiatics and Africans. We can say to them: "We are North Americans, you are South Americans; but we are all Americans, and proud of our homes in this great, glorious and promising continent."

The vastness of Brazil is not fully realized. The geographical maps of South America are usually drawn on a smaller scale than those of the United States, so it is not generally known that the United States of Brazil are larger than the United States of America, exclusive of Alaska and the island possessions. From the most northerly point to the extreme southerly boundary is a distance of two thousand six hundred and seventy-five miles. For the sake of comparison one might say that if our own Atlantic coast line was prolonged in the same way it would reach from the southernmost extremity of Florida to the Hudson Bay region of upper Canada. It extends from four degrees twenty minutes North Latitude to thirty-three degrees forty-five minutes South, or thirty-eight degrees in all. The last ten degrees are below the Tropic of Capricorn and in the temperate zone. From a point near the city of Recife, or Pernambuco, to the most westerly point, is a distance of two thousand seven hundred and twenty-nine miles. From there the country to the south narrows continuously, until it is but a few hundred miles wide in the state of Rio Grande do Sul. A line drawn west from near the city of Bahia, or São Salvador, would give about the medium width. Rio de Janeiro is in longitude nearly half-way across the Atlantic from New York to London, while the easternmost land, Cape San Roque, is still seven hundred miles farther to the east. Within these confines is a territory of three million three hundred and thirty-two thousand seven hundred and thirty square miles, according to the best estimates, and this makes it the fifth country in the world, being exceeded in extent only by China, the British Empire, the United States of America and Russia.

On the South American continent Brazil easily ranks first, as it occupies almost one-half of the entire surface of the continent, and is three times as extensive as its next largest neighbour, the Argentine Republic. The other republics of South America follow in the following order: Colombia, Bolivia, Peru, Venezuela, Chile, Ecuador, Paraguay and Uruguay. The frontiers of this immense republic join those of all the other republics, except Chile, and also touch the borders of British, French and Dutch Guiana, the only foreign possessions on the mainland of this great continent. With one or two little exceptions the boundaries have now been settled by arbitration, so that the future will probably make little change in the limits as now outlined. It is shut off from communication with the Pacific coast by the lofty Andes, and that at least partly accounts for the lack of development in the western part of Brazil. In all, Brazil's coast line amounts to about four thousand miles, all of which is on the Atlantic, and this includes nearly two-thirds of her entire boundary line. It would take a fifteen knot steamer ten days of continuous steaming to travel along this entire coast.

It was a surprise to me to find that it is next to impossible, except in the basin of the Amazon, to get away from the mountains. Hill and valley alternate everywhere, rarely rising to great heights, however, except along the coast, and seldom sinking into great crevasses or cañons. The highest mountain in Brazil, Itatiaia, between Rio de Janeiro and São Paulo, has an altitude of only nine thousand eight hundred and twenty-three feet, while the extreme height of the peaks in most of the ranges seldom exceeds four thousand five hundred feet. The highest range is in general confined to a belt, or chain of mountains, which follows the Atlantic shore, lying at the most but a few miles from the coast, and at times reaching clear to the water's edge, which is known as the Serro da Mar. This range runs from Pernambuco to the borders of Uruguay, so that the coast, wherever seen from the sea, presents only an outline of mountains and serrated peaks, although at the extreme south they scarcely exceed the dignity of hills. The rise from the water's edge is frequently very abrupt, and this has made the problem of railroad construction from the seaports to the interior a difficult as well as expensive proposition.

The broadest plains are probably in the states of Paraná and Rio Grande do Sul, where they assume the appearance of pampas, and it is on those plains that the stock-raising industry has assumed its greatest proportions. Much of the states of Matto Grosso and Amazonas has been practically unexplored, so that the maps of those regions are, for the most part, guesswork, made up from the reports of travellers and amateur scientists, who have written reports of their travels through them. On the government maps one will find the outlines of rivers which are many miles away from the location given them, and the names of towns will appear in the heavy type given only to places of great importance; and yet, if any settlement exists at all at that point, it consists only of a few huts or a little Indian village. Although travellers have visited those sections, the land is untouched by the hand of man, and as virgin as our own western prairies were a half century ago. This land is mostly claimed by families who have never set foot upon it, and yet it has been the cause of deadly feuds among rival claimants; some basing their title upon ancient Portuguese grants, and others upon more recent ones by the republic. There are no roads that can be utilized by commerce, and only the waterways exist to give access to the outside world.

Brazil is a land of great water-courses. It not only has within its borders the greatest river in the world, but it also possesses several rivers which form the chief tributaries of the Rio de la Plata, another of the most extensive fluvial systems in the world. Because of the coast range of mountains nearly all of the water, even from within a few miles of the Atlantic coast, runs hundreds and even thousands of miles north to the Amazon, or south to the La Plata, before finally reaching the ocean. The great amount of the rainfall has made these streams numerous, as well as very broad, as they near their outlet. Between the sources of the two great systems there intervene but two short leagues of swampy ground, which are the common source of the Amazon and the La Plata, the "river of silver," as it is named. The basin of the Amazon is larger than the basin of the Mississippi, the Missouri and many others together. It is as large as two-thirds of our own great land. The amount of water discharged is almost incredible. For hundreds of miles from its mouth the depth sometimes reaches one hundred and fifty feet, and in no place in the channel is it less than sixty feet. Its mouth is wider than the entire length of the lordly Hudson. Ocean steamers run between Iquitos, two thousand five hundred miles from its mouth, and European ports, as well as New York; and many of its tributaries, such as the Madeira and Negro, are mighty rivers in themselves. The Paraná, with its wonderful cascades, and the Uruguay, have their origin in Brazil, and the Paraguay drains many thousands of square miles of her territory. These three rivers form the principal sources of the Rio de la Plata, which carries to the Atlantic Ocean a volume of water exceeded by few rivers in the world.

On the western side of the Atlantic ridge the country forms a series of ridges, or plateaus, making, as some one has characterized it, a colossal stairway. These sudden drops make many fine waterfalls as the waters rush onward toward the Paraná River. The states of São Paulo and Paraná are especially rich in these cascades and rapids, and thus furnish unlimited water power awaiting development. They are no less interesting to the tourist, for nothing in nature is more interesting or fascinating than a fine waterfall, where the waters rush headlong in their precipitous course. The Tietê River alone furnishes many of those cascades, one of them, the Itapura, having a height of forty-four feet. Another is the Urubuhunga, near the former, the water passing over the two being of great volume.

All of these waterfalls, however, are overshadowed by the wonderful falls of the Iguassú, situated on the river of the same name, near its junction with the Paraná River, and on the borders between the republics of Brazil and Argentina. A dozen miles away the smoking columns of mist which crown the falls are plainly visible, and its thunderous roar may sometimes be heard for twenty miles. As one approaches nearer, the mist is more plainly seen and the roar of the waters is heard. The first view of these magnificent falls in their solitary grandeur is inspiring. They have the same general shape as Niagara, and are fifty feet higher. The entire falls are more than two miles in width, with a number of islands dividing the cataract. This may be divided into two sections, the Brazilian and Argentine falls. The head falls are on the Brazilian side and occur on an acute horseshoe bend, somewhat similar to that at Niagara, which is caused by the unequal erosion. Below the falls are depths which a hundred fathom line has failed to sound, and the natives call them bottomless. There is a triple leap of three hundred and twenty feet, the last one alone being a drop of two hundred and thirteen feet over sheer precipices of dark rock. At the present time it is difficult of access, because it is reached by ascending the Rio de la Plata and Paraná River, a journey of almost two weeks, or by a several days' journey overland from Ponta Grossa, in the state of Paraná. Some day, when the means of communication become better, it will no doubt be visited by thousands of people each season. It still remains in all its primitive beauty, for the hand of man has as yet done nothing to detract from or add to what nature herself created. It is like another Niagara set out in the midst of a wilderness, with dense lines of waving bamboo or other trees marking the boundaries of the stream. Like Tennyson's *Brook*, the Iguassú might say:

> "For men may come and men may go,
>   But I go on forever."

FALLS OF IGUASSÚ.

Above these falls on the Paraná are the wonderful Guayra falls, one hundred and twenty-five miles above the junction with the Iguassú; and four hundred miles still farther up are the Uberaponga falls, with many smaller cataracts intervening. Below Guayra cataract the current piles up in the centre with a corkscrew action, and then dives down again into midstream. It returns to the surface in eddies which leap up twelve or fifteen feet in the air, making, as one scientific investigator terms it, "rapids with which the whirlpool rapids of Niagara are a quiet duckpond in comparison." One is lost in considering this frantic water power here awaiting the harnessing by man.

Of the climate of Brazil much has been said in a disparaging way. It has been classed as a tropical country, and therefore subject to all the ills supposed to be connected with such a climate. And yet the climate is so varied that the subject can not be dismissed in a single paragraph. It is hot in places, but even in Rio de Janeiro the evenings are generally very pleasant and comfortable, the thermometer usually going down to about sixty degrees Fahrenheit. At least one can always find it so by establishing his home a few hundred feet above the sea level, on one of the adjacent hills. I doubt if the people of Rio suffer from the oppressively hot nights as much as New Yorkers or Chicagoans, and I was there in December, supposed to be one of the hottest months. Fifteen hundred to two thousand feet above the sea level the climate is really delightful, and one need not pity the people who dwell there. Some one has said that the whole country might be compared to a beautiful Tennessee, without the rigours of winter. Along the Amazon it is hot and humid, and yet I have met Englishmen who had lived in Manaos and Pará for years, and who sighed to go back to those places because they loved the climate. In the southern states of Paraná and Rio Grande do Sul the climate is about the same as Argentina, which is regarded as temperate.

There is plenty of rainfall everywhere except in two or three states, almost underneath the equator. On the Atlantic coast it ranges from one hundred to two hundred inches annually. Along the Amazon it is much greater, and on the inland plateaus it will probably average seventy-five inches per year. Thus, in the vast area of Brazil, almost every variety of climate will be found, except the extreme cold, which is absent. It used to be thought that people could not live so near the equator, but proper hygiene takes away all danger of the so-called tropical diseases, so dreaded by most people from colder climes.

As one writer has well said: "Diseases in cold climates are always looked upon as calamities quite independent of climatic conditions; even if ignorant of their causes, pathologists always had an explanation ready. In the case of warm countries, it is otherwise. Without any further inquiry the climate has been blamed as the enemy. The European nations drew around themselves sanitary cordons of quarantine and disinfection against cholera, yellow fever and plague, and for a long time never thought of going right to the source of trouble and improving sanitary conditions in the countries where these diseases had their origin."

It has really been a base libel upon these countries to blame everything upon the climate and climatic conditions. The heat and humidity may make some diseases more fatal, but at the same time they seem to act as preventative to others which are far more fatal in colder climates. The United States taught the world this lesson at Havana and in Panama, and it has been a valuable one for the world. Brazil has wakened up to this necessity, and now Santos, Bahia, and other cities, as well as the capital, have followed a cleaning-up policy that has brought the death-rate down to where it will compare favourably with other cities of the world.

The United States of Brazil is a republic very much like the United States of America in form. Its constitution is modelled after that of the United States, a Portuguese translation of which was made for them. It differs, however, in some respects. A president, for instance, is ineligible to succeed himself; and even a vice-president, who has succeeded to the presidency, can not be a candidate for that office without a term intervening. The power of the national government is less than that of our own, and the state has greater importance. This condition was made almost necessary in the formation of the republic in order to gain the adherence of many of the states, as they aimed to get as far away from the centralization idea as possible. The great distances separating them likewise, and slow communication between them, has encouraged these differences. In many respects the state governments are too powerful, and the national government too weak. Each state has its own army, although in a measure subject to the national government, but this local militia is more loyal to the state than the national government. The unoccupied land is the property of the various states, instead of the national government as with us, and this has contributed in making the state governments of unusual importance.

The republic is composed of twenty states, one territory and the Federal District, in which is situated the national capital. The states are very uneven in size, the largest being Amazonas, with more than a million square miles of territory, one-third of the whole, and Sergipe having only about twenty-five thousand square miles. Out of the total population of about eighteen million, more than one-fifth live in the state of Minas Geraes, while the great state of Amazonas contains only about one person for each five square miles of territory. The state of Matto Grosso, second in size and also colossal, has even a smaller ratio of population, according to the statistics, which are probably not very accurate on these little known states. São Paulo has heretofore been the most powerful state, and Rio Grande do Sul has had the most checkered history, for its German inhabitants have not always been in harmony or sympathy with the Latins, who predominate in the other states, and they have maintained several uprisings on their own account.

The republic was established on the 15th of November, 1889, and there have been six presidents elected. The term of office is four years. A vice-president is elected who serves in the event of the death or incapacity of the President; the present President having succeeded to the office on the death of Dr. Affonso Augusto Moreira Penna, in June, 1909. The National Assembly is composed of a Senate and House of Deputies. Each state and the federal capital are entitled to three senators who serve for nine years, and a deputy is allowed for each seventy thousand inhabitants, with a minimum of four for any state. The congress now consists of sixty-three senators and two hundred and fifteen deputies, one-third of the former being elected every three years. Each state has its own president, congress, cabinet and other officials, almost identical with the federal officials. The qualifications for suffrage are quite generous; but only a small proportion of those qualified actually vote at the elections, which are always held on Sunday, and generally in the churches. It is safe to say that on those days the religious services do not claim much attention. There is generally a clique, or oligarchy, in each state, which dominates political affairs. These men absolutely dictate the matters of the state and represent the affairs of that state in national politics. Corruption is quite a common thing, but that the farther up one goes the less of it is to be found is my belief. The several presidential administrations have been good, but many of the municipal administrations have followed crooked paths openly.

"*Ordem e Progreso*," order and progress, is the motto of the Republic of Brazil. The flag consists of a green rectangle, representing the vegetable kingdom, with a diamond-shaped yellow block in the centre, representing the mineral wealth. In the centre is a blue circle, which corresponds with the blue of the skies, with the above motto across it. Within the blue circle are twenty-one stars, representing the twenty states and federal district, five of which are grouped to represent the constellation of the Southern Cross. The coat of arms contains the same colours and emblems arranged in an artistic design, and with some other insignia added.

The developed part of Brazil is only a small part of the whole country. It constitutes a fringe along the Atlantic coast, and bears about the same relation to the whole country as the original thirteen states do to the United States as at present constituted. There are few large cities, but numerous small towns of from five to twenty thousand, and many villages are scattered over the land. No part is overpopulated, the most densely populated being the states of Alagoas and Rio de Janeiro, with an average of perhaps twenty-three to the square mile, and there is no danger of even those states being overpopulated for some time yet. In a land where all the year around is a growing season this is a very small population, even considering the mountainous character of most of the country. If peopled as densely as France, Brazil would have a population of not less than three hundred and twenty million. It is almost purely an agricultural country, although some advancement has been made in manufactures through government encouragement and high customs duties. Especially has this been true in cotton goods, and there are many small factories of these textiles scattered over the land, most of them run by the water power which is so abundant in most sections. Some other factories have been started through concessions being granted, but by far the greatest part of the goods used are imported from the manufacturing nations of the world. This governmental assistance causes many of the factories to feel that to some extent they are government enterprises. The same policy has been followed with railroads of guaranteeing returns instead of making grants of lands, which would be an incentive to the railroad to aid in development. The São Paulo-Rio Grande Railway is one exception to this rule, and it is prospering. The Central Railroad, which has over a thousand miles of main track, is owned and operated as a government institution, and this method has not been a success any more than the Lloyd Brazilian line of national steamers. Money goes in from all sources, but the government treasury is compelled every year to make up deficits.

Brazil was discovered in the year 1500 by the Portuguese navigator Pedro Alvares Cabral, who took possession of it in the name of his sovereign. It was first named Terra de Santa Cruz, the Land of the Holy Cross, but the name was changed to that of the dyewood which had been in use before. The French soon after began to trade with the natives, but they were driven off by the Portuguese. The Huguenots of the country likewise attempted to establish a free religious colony at what is now Rio de Janeiro, but this attempt was also frustrated, and Rio did not become an important place until the middle of the eighteenth century. The Jesuits sought to make a religious settlement out of São Paulo, but the energetic "Paulistas" rose in their might and drove them into the Spanish territories.

The Portuguese began to colonize the country, and established a number of settlements along the coast. Pernambuco was founded in 1526 and Bahia in 1549, as compared with New York in 1614 and Boston in 1621. The country was divided into fifteen capitancias, each with fifty leagues of coast, and stretching inland in parallel lines to the westernmost limits of the country. These were granted by the king to Portuguese nobles. Numerous struggles took place with the Spaniards, who tried to seize all of South America, and were in actual control of nearly all of the rest of the South American coast. The political outline was finally determined by natural configurations. The Portuguese kept in control of the district penetrated by the Amazon and its tributaries, as far as they were navigable, and the Spaniards got control as far as the Rio de la Plata was navigable on the south; and between these two boundaries the land was kept in the hands of the Portuguese. Where navigation was impeded on the Paraguay, Paraná and Uruguay Rivers, there Spanish domination ended. On the remainder of the coast the Spaniards maintained their supremacy, except the small Dutch, French and English settlements in Guiana. It speaks well for the indomitable perseverance of a small country like Portugal that they acquired and maintained for three centuries such a vast empire, when the mother country is smaller than one island at the mouth of the Amazon.

When King John brought his court over to Brazil, in 1809, a national spirit was engendered. After he returned to Portugal, it was not long until an independent spirit arose and revolution was in the air. Then came a new-world empire, during which the Dom Pedros, I and II, reigned. Each was expelled from the country; the first with rejoicing, the second with sadness, and, perhaps, many a tear. When one considers that the republic only reaches its majority in this year of 1910, and that slavery was abolished only twenty-two years ago, both of these changes being accomplished without bloodshed, the progress of the country can be better understood, and many of its shortcomings more easily overlooked. Furthermore the early advance of the country was stunted by the lust for gold of the first Portuguese colonists. Everything was sacrificed to immediate results, in order that they might return to the homeland and live in luxury. It was different from the motive that influenced either Puritan or Cavalier in our own land, for they sought liberty. The evil effects of this early exploitation have been felt during the intervening centuries, not alone in Brazil, but throughout all of South America.

CHAPTER II
ALONGTHECOASTT OTHECAPIT AL

It is a delightful journey of a little more than two weeks from New York to the capital of Brazil. In a little more than twenty-four hours after leaving that metropolis, even in the middle of the winter, the vessel is ploughing through balmy seas, and the passengers are sitting on the spacious decks of the comfortable steamers with all wraps discarded. As the route of these steamers is east of that of vessels bound for the Caribbean seas, few boats are sighted, and day after day is passed without the sight of a sail. For thirteen days our ship, the *Vasari*, sailed through stormless waters, with only one full-rigged schooner coming within our horizon, and no land to be seen.

It was not until near the equator that even a rain storm clouded the skies, and then fleeting showers chased each other across the skies, and peals of thunder and flashes of lightning occasionally created a diversion. The sunsets were wonderful. As evening approached, dark clouds seemed to gather near the horizon; the sun slowly approached them, and then dropped suddenly out of sight. Streaks of red and crimson, silver and gold shot out, and these diffused and melted into each other with the constant variations of the kaleidoscope. The contrast of bright hues with the dark, ominous-looking clouds was striking. There was no twilight, and darkness immediately followed. It was the time of the full moon also. Just a little while after the setting of the sun the moon would rise on the opposite side of the boat. An immense and luminous ball the Queen of the Night appeared, and rapidly climbed up over the bank of clouds; and then, as it dwindled in size, it increased in brilliancy, until the dancing waves were covered with a silvery sheen. Never have I seen such beautiful scenes as we witnessed for several nights when near the equatorial line.

Watches were changed each day since we were constantly travelling eastward, as one will see by consulting a map. New York is situated in longitude seventy-four degrees west, while the easternmost coast of Brazil is in longitude thirty-five degrees west. At last the sandy shores of Rio

Grande do Norte are sighted, and the vessel rounds Cape San Roque. Far out at sea little sails appear in considerable numbers, and when near enough to see them it is found that they are simply rafts made of logs fastened together. These are the "catamaran" fishing boats, from the port of Pernambuco. The adventurous boatmen will sometimes venture out a hundred miles to sea in these simple and frail-looking crafts, and they are seldom lost.

Pernambuco, or Recife, is the first port at which the transatlantic steamers stop, and it is either here, or at Bahia, that the American traveller down the east coast first sets his foot on Brazilian soil. It is the second city of importance in northeastern Brazil, and the state of Pernambuco, of which it is the capital, is second in importance only to Bahia. Recife is nearer to Europe than any other South American port, and it is usually made the first port of call by the many steamers which ply to that continent. A coral reef extends along the shore, and at a distance of a few hundred feet from it, thus making a natural harbour for vessels that are not of too deep draught; and it is this reef that gives the name to the city, for Recife means a reef. It is a natural wall rising straight up out of the water, on the top of which has been built a low wall of stone. At high tide this wall is generally high enough to keep out the sea. Recife is a busy port and a great shipping port for sugar, as that is the particular product of this state. The influence of the early Dutch colonists here can still be traced in the old buildings. One finds in travelling through Brazil that each state has only one principal production, which supports the people, and the export tax on which provides the government with funds. At one time this state had a monopoly in sugar production and Pernambuco sugar was known the world over.

THE MUNICIPAL THEATRE, PERNAMBUCO.

Recife is divided into three parts by streams of water or lagoons, and there are many bridges connecting the various parts. In fact it is cut up so much by these arms of the ocean that it has been called the South American Venice. The city is fifth in size in the republic, and is quite a pretty little city with plazas and parks after the usual style. In the oldest part of the city the streets are narrow and crooked, but on the other and larger peninsula, the blocks of houses are larger, the streets wider, and there are some good stores as well as tram cars. The colour of the inhabitants is rather marked, but there is, possibly, not so large a percentage of the negro element as in the larger city lower down on the coast.

The state of Pernambuco is a state about the size of Ohio, and one of the important states in the republic. Its population exceeds the million mark. Because of its large black population, many of whom were formerly slaves, education has not advanced here as much as in a number of the states farther south. Its commerce is considerable, with sugar as the leading item. Cotton is also an important production. At the port one can see cotton coming in on wagons, ox-carts, the backs of mules and even on the black shoulders of the inhabitants. The coast-line of Pernambuco is only a little over a hundred miles in length, but the state runs inland for several hundred miles.

It will probably be surprising to many people to know that the whaling industry is quite an important one along this coast, for this sport is supposed to be confined to polar waters. And yet I have personally seen whales on the western coast of South America almost as far north as the equator. On this coast they are caught up to within twelve degrees of the line. Along the coast of Bahia there are several whaling stations, most of which are in the vicinity of the city of Bahia. As soon as the Antarctic winter sets in, the whales begin to migrate northward and reach these waters in May. From then until November the whaling boats may be seen at any time out on the Atlantic with all sails set, looking for a "blow," which marks the presence of the game. Passengers on the steamers also watch for the same signs, as it is a novel sight to those making their first trip, and the older travellers are also looking for any diversion.

The whales caught are full of blubber, but the whalebone in the jaws of the variety found here is too short to have much commercial value. The whales generally average from thirty to fifty feet in length, but catches are sometimes made of these marine monsters that will reach sixty feet long. The longest one of which any record has been made was seventy feet from its nose to the end of its tail, and yielded nearly six thousand quarts of oil. The meat is also considered quite a delicacy by many of the Bahians, who devour it eagerly. The methods pursued by the whaler are primitive, and more than half the whales once harpooned finally escape. And yet with all this primitiveness, the average annual catch is from three to four hundred whales, which is not such a bad record.

A day's run brings the traveller to the most important city in Brazil north of Rio de Janeiro. It is situated on a bay which is generally classed as one of the fine harbours of the world. When Americus Vespucius entered this beautiful and commodious harbour with a fleet, he named it Bahia da Todos os Santos, the Bay of All Saints, in honour of the feast day on which it was first seen. When this discovery was reported to the King of Portugal, he sent out an expedition with instructions to build a city "strong enough not only to keep the natives in awe, but also to resist the attack of any more formidable army." The present city was founded in 1549, so that the city has outgrown its swaddling clothes long ago. It has also been a city of importance, as it was for almost two centuries the seat of colonial power, and the residence of the Governor-General representing the Crown. The city was originally named São Salvador, and should be called that to-day, but the name of the state clings to the capital as well.

The bay up which the vessel sails to its anchorage has sheltered many and strange craft during the past four centuries since its first discovery. It is a magnificent expanse of water, completely sheltered from the open sea, and large enough to contain all the navies of the world, for it is from ten to twenty miles wide and twenty-seven miles in length. There are no docks, and the boat generally anchors about half a mile from shore. As soon as the port officer has visited the ship, a gang of bandits in the form of men of dark visage crowd around the gangway, and seek to take the passengers ashore. It is necessary to bargain very carefully, and pay nothing to the boatman until the round trip has been made; otherwise you will be compelled to pay extra for your return to the ship.

The city is divided into an upper and a lower town, and is quite an imposing place. The lower part is a narrow, sun-baked strip along the sea front, and is devoted to the shipping and banking interests. One would think that even they would want to get away from the foul-smelling odours which prevail along the waterfront. As one writer has said, "there is a distinct and separate bad smell to every house."

THE BOAT LANDING, BAHIA.

During the day this section is a busy place, but at night a funereal quiet prevails. The upper city, or *Cidade Alta*, is reached by a long winding road, or by means of the ascensors, or elevators, of which there are several. The upper city is composed of broader streets, is in every way more attractive, and the air seems much purer and sweeter than in the lower town.

The sights are novel enough, too, especially if it is the first Brazilian city visited. Here one will also meet with that luxuriant growth of flowers, which are seen in every plaza and private dooryard. The public buildings, of which there are a number, for this city is the capital of a state as large as California, are very creditable. The governor's palace, the senate building, the municipal and other buildings occupy conspicuous sites. There are many churches, of which the Cathedral is the most interesting, and is one of the oldest buildings in the country, having originally been built as a Jesuit college. Clubs, theatres and bathing resorts also add a liveliness to life in this city. Bahia has always been known for its noted names in literature, and many of the brightest men in Brazilian arts and letters were natives of this state.

The bright hues of the buildings add a brilliance of colour to the city which some one has described as "mashed rainbows." There are vivid yellow, green, purple, sky blue, terra-cotta and many other equally striking shades. Many of the buildings are covered with porcelain tiles, which render them very attractive. Some of the windows are ornamented with a lace work of wrought iron, and occasionally the decoration over the doors is of the same metal, which is said to be of negro designing. Some of these houses date back to colonial times, but others have more cosmopolitan characteristics. The fronts of the yards are ornamented with flowering trees and shrubs that harmonize (in some instances) with the bright colours adorning the plaster covering of the adobe brick, which is the basis of construction used here. Most of the houses are only one story, although two stories are fairly common, and occasionally a sky-scraper three stories in height may be encountered.

There is one thing that will impress itself upon the traveller, and that is the colour of its inhabitants, for it is said that Bahia has a greater proportion of negroes than any other Brazilian city, but it would be a close race between that city and Pernambuco. One might think that he had stepped into one of our southern states, except for the fact that none of the kinky-haired inhabitants speak English. All of them jabber in the guttural Portuguese. Everywhere one goes there are negroes, and negroes of every hue from the aboriginal blackness to a chocolate brown and saffron yellow. I counted fifty people as they passed by me on one of the principal streets. Of this number forty-five were decidedly black, three were surely white, and the remaining two I was not certain about. At the same time a fellow-traveller counted thirty-five on the other side of the street, and said that he was sure of only two white people out of that number. This was about the middle of the day, when the white people were probably taking their siesta, and the proportion would not hold good over the whole city. It is certain, however, as statistics show, that at least eighty per cent. of the population have a sprinkling of negro blood in their veins. And yet, with all this preponderance of blacks, the attempt of the United States to appoint a negro consul at this port almost raised a tropical hurricane just a few years ago.

The shade of black does not mean social ostracism, and one will find white and black side by side in every social circle. Along the docks, and in the markets, one may see the negro men bearing heavy burdens on their heads, after the manner of Mexican cargadors, while the women sit around with a few articles for sale, and smoke huge, black cigars while waiting for prospective customers. The women also have that peculiar stride, which is characteristic of those who are accustomed to carry loads upon their heads. Some of the negro women are monstrous in size, and weigh from two hundred to two hundred and fifty pounds. Their dress, which consists of a long, white sleeveless chemise cut low in the neck, is so simple that it is easy to see that no padding is used. Nearly all wear white, or brightly coloured turbans, some wear shawls folded across the shoulders, and all are either barefooted or wear a heelless slipper.

The shacks made of lumps of clay thrust between slats like lath, and roofed with thatch, which one may find on the edge of the city, are the homes of many of these improvident blacks. In this climate there is no need to lay up for to-morrow, and children are not expensive, for clothing is not needed until several years after they become members of the family. Some of the poor babies may wear a simple coin or chain around the neck, but that will be all, except perhaps the innocent smile of childhood. And yet most of these negroes seemed to be busy at something, although the wages earned are no doubt very small. They impressed me as being rather superior in type to many of our negroes, such as one may find in some parts of Mississippi or Alabama.

It is not good policy for a white man to appear on the street without a coat, as he will lay himself liable to insult by the negroes. One of the men from the steamer took off his coat and carried it on his arm. A white man warned him, but he did not understand the language. It was not long until some negroes began to throw things at him. As soon as he put his coat on again these insults stopped. Coatless comfort on hot days is reserved by the negroes themselves.

The breath of the tropics prevails at Bahia, as it is not far from the equatorial line. A ride to the suburb of Rio Vermelho, which looks out upon the sea, passes through avenues of tropical trees and past fields of bananas. To me the palm is the most interesting tree of the tropics. The mango with its dense foliage, the umbrella tree with its curious yet graceful shape, and many flowering trees—all of these are beautiful; but when I see the palm, I feel like saying with the poet:

> "I love the Palm
> With his leaves of beauty, his fruit of balm."

Tropical fruits of many kinds grow in abundance. The Bahia oranges, which are green in colour, have a fine flavour. The cajú is a peculiar fruit about the size of a lemon, with the seed growing out at one end, as though it was stuck on in some way. This fruit is sweet but astringent, and is considered a great blood purifier. The kidney-shaped nut, when raw, is dangerous to eat because of poisonous juice it contains; but a roasting drives out the poisonous quality and the nut is then delicious. The mango, which, to those who have cultivated a liking, is the most delicious of fruits, grows to great size in Bahia, and has a most excellent flavour. One feels like getting into a bathtub, however, after eating one, in order to get rid of the muss made in eating it. I have not yet learned to be fond of this tropical fruit for, like olives, the taste is acquired, and it oftentimes requires many and repeated efforts to cultivate a taste. There is a fruit that grows out of the side and trunk of great trees, which much resembles an immense hedge apple, that is peculiar to this district. It grows to an immense size, and the natives are very fond of it. Then there are melons called the mammão, that grow on trees, and which much resemble the cantaloupe in appearance, but differ in flavour. This melon is said to have excellent digestive properties because of the abundance of pepsin which it contains. All of these, and many more novel things one will find in the markets. The curious little marmosette monkeys, which are not much larger than a good-sized rat, are very common. Then again, this is the home of talking parrots, and their shrill screeches are heard from almost every doorway.

The first experience of the traveller with Brazilian money is rather amusing. In New York I had obtained five thousand five hundred reis, which seemed like a large sum of money, enough to pay for the whole trip. Imagine my surprise when I found it lacked five hundred reis of enough to pay for my first meal on shore! It cost three hundred reis to mail a letter to the States, and a street car ride cost another four hundred reis. My boatman cheated me out of one thousand reis without moving an eyelid. All of these things caused me to put pencil to paper in a little calculation. I found that I was a millionaire for the first time in my life. At the rate of exchange then prevailing three hundred and twenty-five dollars would buy one million reis, the money of the country. You may feel like a millionaire when the bank clerk hands over to you a package of bills, with thousands of reis printed all over them; but the illusion soon vanishes when your hotel bill is presented after a few days' stay, for a million reis soon disappears. The reis in an infinitesimal coin, so small that you could scarcely see it with a magnifying glass, for one thousand of them are worth only thirty-one cents. The milreis (one thousand reis) is used as the unit, and accounts are thus carried in the decimal system, with the dollar mark at the end of the thousand. Thus, one million reis, which is one thousand milreis, or, as it is generally called, one conto, would be written 1,000$000. It is the same as the Portuguese monetary system, although the Brazilian milreis is only worth about half as much as that of Portugal. The money is all paper, and the most of it is the dirtiest and filthiest money I have ever handled. Some of the bills are so tattered, torn and greasy that it is almost impossible for a stranger to tell what denomination they are. The small denominations are large and awkward coins of several different issues, and of several different sizes.

The state of Bahia is one of the larger states of Brazil, and has a coast line of several hundred miles. It is traversed by mountains in every direction, and that has perhaps been the cause of the tardy development of the country through railroad construction, because of the difficulties and expenses involved. There are a couple of railways which run inland from Bahia, but no railroad connects it with the adjoining states. It is always necessary to come back to the capital city, and take the steamer again for whatever port one is bound for. The productions of the state are varied, and a great deal of the products is exported. The tobacco export from this port is greater than that of all the other productions together. The leaf tobacco is exported in great quantities, but the Bahia cigarettes and cigars have a great reputation in Brazil; and the manufacture of them furnishes employment to thousands of the dusky-hued Bahians. When you consider that the women aid the men in smoking, it will be seen that the home consumption is no inconsiderable quantity.

A dusky boatman rowed me out to the vessel, just as the sun was setting in a lurid glow behind the hills, which form the background of Bahia. The dancing waves reflected the lurid colours of the retreating sun, and the bright colours of the Bahia houses seemed to be borrowed from that radiant orb. Then, as darkness fell, the electric lights were lighted in the lower town and up on the hill; and Bahia looked like a city of enchantment. Here and there moved streaks of light as the electric cars dashed along; and again, similar streaks moved up and down as the ascensors carried their loads. Rockets were going up in various parts of the city, for some religious celebration was being held. It was amidst such scenes that our good ship weighed anchor and we moved south, getting farther and farther away from the fierce breath of the tropics at each revolution of the rapidly revolving propeller.

RIO DE JANEIRO. LOOKING ACROSS THE BAY AT SUGAR LOAF.

With land in sight about half the time, it was almost a three days' journey to cover the intervening distance of seven hundred and fifty miles to Rio de Janeiro. On the morning of the third day the passengers were on deck early, for the capital was nearing. The sandy shores of the mainland were visible, with their background of rugged peaks. Little rocky islands with the surf dashing up against their jagged edges rose out of the water, and were successively passed. Schools of fish that swam so near to the surface, that they could be followed by the agitation of the water which they caused, were chased by flocks of birds that ever and anon dashed beneath the surface and came up with their prey. As the morning fog lifted, curious forts with disappearing guns could be outlined on the shore, and one imposing fort on a prominent peak seemed to protect the city. Then old Sugar Loaf, which has been so much pictured, lifted its lofty head out of the gloom, with Corcovado and the other peaks in the background. Gradually the harbour of Rio de Janeiro, which is said by all travellers to be one of the most beautiful, if not the most beautiful bay in the world, unfolded itself; and back of the blue waters of the bay were the white walls and red-tiled roofs of the city, and above and beyond the city were the fantastic peaks of the many oddly formed hills which form the background of this fascinating city.

There are a number of other states in this section of Brazil, each of which deserves some mention. Between Pernambuco and Bahia lie two of the smaller states, Alagoas and Sergipe. The former is a state almost as large as Indiana, and is the most populous in the republic. It is a rich agricultural state, with sugar and cotton as the principal crops. The name, A-lagoas, means the lakes, and it is upon one of the principal of these that the capital, Maceio, is situated. This is a pretty little town of forty thousand or more inhabitants. The people of the state are generally Portuguese, with more or less mixture of the native or negro races. The two military presidents of Brazil were from this state. Sergipe, the smallest state, is nearly twice as large as our own state of Massachusetts, and has a population of about half a million. On the coast it is low, hot and swampy, but in the interior the soil is higher, and most of it very fertile. It has neither a railroad nor a good port, so that the state is greatly handicapped in its commerce. The capital is Aracajú, which is a pretty little tropical city of about twenty-five thousand people. It is quite probable that Sergipe will one day be absorbed by one of the larger states, as the financial problem is a serious one.

Sections of each of the three states lying north of Pernambuco, Parahyba, Rio Grande do Norte and Ceará lie within what is termed an arid belt. This seems a very strange occurrence so near the equator. There are, however, droughts there that last for several years, and so greatly impoverish the people that government succour becomes necessary. When I was in Brazil a government commission was just starting for that section to study the question, and see what could be done to introduce dry farming methods. Parahyba, which is a little larger than Alagoas, is perhaps the least affected, but still its climate is generally hot and dry. In the lowlands sugar and rice are cultivated, and in the uplands cereals. Cotton is likewise one of the chief products, and a great many cattle are raised in the interior. The capital city has the same name, and is an interior town connected with the seaport, Cabedello, by rail.

Rio Grande do Norte is the most northeasterly state, and was the first land sighted by Europeans on the shores of South America. Its area of twenty-two thousand square miles includes much arid territory where rain is very uncertain. Artesian wells have been tried without much success, and dry farming seems to be the only hope, although the droughts only come periodically. Premiums have been offered for the digging of these wells, and the construction of dams or reservoirs. One of the chief industries outside of agriculture is the production of salt, of which thousands of tons are made each year from the rich saline deposits along the northern shore. Natal is the capital and chief seaport. Although this city is not large to-day, it is very old, having been founded in 1597.

Ceará is a progressive state despite famines which have come about every eleven years, and at times have greatly reduced the population, for fevers have generally followed the famines. The inhabitants are workers, and from this state have been drawn the labourers to develop the rubber industry. Ceará was the first state to emancipate the slaves, and in many ways the people have shown themselves progressive. They stick to the home land regardless of famines and droughts, and cultivate their fields assiduously. The cacao of this state is very fine, and the cattle industry is an important one. This state, the size of Illinois, supports a population of nearly a million, of which about fifty thousand live in the capital city of Fortaleza.

Piauhy is a large state about which little is known. It has a population of less than two to the square mile, and has a coast line not exceeding ten miles on the Atlantic. Only a very small portion of the land is cultivated. The principal exports are a white wax, made from the scales of a palm, and a rubber known as Maniçoba rubber. The towns are small, the largest, Therizina, also the capital, having a population of only twenty thousand. There is much fine timber in the state, and probably not a saw-mill to cut it. With railroads, men of enterprise and money, Piauhy might be developed into a great, prosperous and influential state.

About half-way between Bahia and Pernambuco is the mouth of the São Francisco River, another of the great water-courses of Brazil. For a thousand miles from its mouth this river is navigable for small vessels, except for a distance of about one hundred miles, where there are some wonderful rapids and inspiring falls. In April, when the dry season sets in, the people from the hillsides and mountains move down to plant their corn, beans, rice and mandioca. The freshets leave a deposit of fine white sand, which enriches the soil. It is not necessary to break the ground. The native makes a hole in the ground, with a sharp stick, into which a seed is dropped and then covered. He then builds a shelter of the palm branches and awaits the maturing of his crops. When they are gathered he sells his surplus to the traders, and moves up again into the hills and mountains, where he lives a life of comparative ease and idleness until the next season.

THE PAULO AFFONSO FALLS.

The principal falls of the São Francisco are called Paulo Alfonso, and are a two days' trip up the river from its mouth, through tropical scenery. The average width of this river above the falls is two-thirds of a mile, and the volume of water is great, for it drains an immense territory. The rapids begin some distance above the falls proper. The whirling and churning water is dashed along on its way toward the final leap, where this immense volume of water is forced through a break in the precipitous banks, not more than fifty feet wide. The falls are slightly crescent shaped. As the main body of the water rushes, leaps and surges down the steep incline of the last rapids, it is hurled against a steep black wall with great momentum; broken into foam and spray, swishing, swirling and churning, it then rebounds only to be pushed over the abyss at a right angle to its original course. The waters then rush forward for a few hundred feet, only to be hurled back by another rock wall three hundred feet high, thus forming a whirlpool, from which it finally escapes and passes through a narrow gorge for several miles, from which it emerges in a little quieter mood. The total fall of the water is two hundred and seventy feet. The view from a height of nearly one hundred feet, as one looks down upon the final leap of one hundred and ninety feet, is awe-inspiring. There is not only a wonderful view of the falls from that point, but a bird's-eye view of the rapids, and the roar of the falls and rapids is something terrific.

CHAPTER III
THE CITY OF BEAUTIFUL VIEWS

If the capital of Argentina deserves to be called the "City of Good Airs," then the capital of Brazil should be termed Buenas Vistas, the "City of Beautiful Views." Of all the cities in the world Rio de Janeiro best deserves to be called by that name. This is not my opinion alone, but it is the almost unanimous verdict of this most beautiful city. Everywhere that the eye falls, it is met with a view that is a worthy subject for the artist's brush. The camera fiend is kept busy "pressing the button," for at almost every turn there is the temptation to expose the sensitive plate which will reproduce the scene that so appeals to the eye. But, although the plate or film faithfully reproduces the outline and detail of the scene, the blue of the sky and the waters of the bay, the green of the palms, and the other trees, the colours of the flowers which are omnipresent, and the bright and varied tints of the houses are sadly missing in the resulting photograph. All of these are absolutely necessary to complete the picture, which lingers in the memory of one who has visited this second city of South America.

When the early navigators sailed up the island-studded bay, which leads to the present site of the capital of Brazil, they thought it must surely be the mouth of a broad river, and, as it was in the month of January, they named it, for want of a better name, Rio de Janeiro, the River of January, and the name has clung to the bay and settlement, which has grown into a thriving city, during the succeeding four centuries. No one, however, since that time has been able to discover the supposed river which led to the name. So this city of lovely views and of romantic history bears, and has always borne, a name which is a misnomer, but this fact has not affected either the beauty of the scene or the development of the city. It is simply another illustration of the saying that there is little in a name, and a rose by any other name would smell just as sweet. The inhabitant of the city is even called a "flumenense," from the word meaning a river.

The full name of Brazil's capital is San Sebastian de Rio de Janeiro, and its foundation dates back to the year 1566, when a landing was effected here by a few colonists near the famous Sugar Loaf mountain. A citadel was built on a hill now called Morro do Castillo. Near this was next erected a church called San Sebastian, in honour of the city's patron saint, which ancient structure is still standing as one of the few memorials of the remote past, and within its walls rest the remains of the city's founder, Estacio de Sá. There are still a few other relics of these earlier days, but most of them have been greatly altered, and many of them practically rebuilt.

For a couple of centuries Brazil was the seat of Portuguese power in the new world, and it was the centre of many political struggles during the capitancias. It pulsated with that excitement that can only be found in Latin cities, and many a plot and counterplot has been batched within its environs. For a while, during Napoleon's occupancy of the throne, it was the seat of government, for the royal family of Portugal fled to these hospitable shores, and all the wealth, pomp, splendour and gayety of a powerful and extravagant court was transferred to this city. This lasted only for a short time, for Napoleon was overthrown, and the royal family returned to the mother land. Political discontent in Brazil soon led to the establishment of an independent empire, with the son of the reigning monarch of Portugal as the ruler of the new nation.

Rio, for nearly every one uses the short appellation, has seen many changes. Starting as a small settlement of adventurers, it became successively the capital of a capitancia, a province, a kingdom, an empire and a republic. All of the latter changes have taken place within the last century. And yet, among all those changes, from the extreme of capitancia to republic, there has been none which so completely affected the appearance, and perhaps final destiny of the city, as the metamorphosis which has taken place during the past half dozen years. The visitor to the Rio of a decade ago, with its antiquated streets, old-fashioned architecture and foul-smelling open-sewered public thoroughfares, which more nearly resembled alleys than streets, would scarcely recognize the new capital of broad avenues, clean, well-swept pavements and the beautiful boulevard which follows the sweep of the bay for many miles.

AVENIDA CENTRAL, RIO DE JANEIRO.

The old has not been entirely displaced by the new, for the famous Ouvidor still remains, and during all the business hours of the day is filled with a throng of shoppers, business men and the idle who spend their waking hours in the cafés or other resorts. It is still the great shopping as well as gossiping street. The people spread themselves over the sidewalk and street, for all other traffic is excluded from this street during those hours. It still possesses some of the best stores and the best of everything that pleases the Brazilians. Thousands of people pass through this street each day, who come for no other purpose than to shake hands with and talk to friends. It may be that their only desire is to see and to be seen. The officeholder comes here to feel the pulse of the people, and the politician tries to hold a public reception on the sidewalk. It is likewise a cosmopolitan crowd, for one will find not only all classes of Brazilians, but many other nationalities. Swells with silk hats bump up against half-dressed negroes with loads on their heads. Lottery peddlers accost you on every corner, and sometimes pester you until it becomes an annoyance. Many of the other streets might be recognized as they have not been changed, although the nomenclature is different, for there has been a new set of heroes and notables, whose names should be preserved in this public way. Nearly all of the old names have disappeared from the signs that face the traveller on all the corners. Even on old Ouvidor, instead of that familiar word, appears in places the name of Moreira Cesar. Other new names are 15th of November, 7th of September, Gonçalves Diaz (the poet), etc., etc.

A few years ago the city fathers decided that they would transform the capital and make it not only a beautiful but a more beautiful city. Engineers and architects were employed, plans were drawn up and work was begun on an elaborate scale, which has not been entirely completed as yet. Perhaps the most remarkable feature of the work was the construction of the Avenida Central through the centre of the city, from sea to sea, and its continuation around the bay where it is called Avenida Beira Mar. The Avenida Central starts at a section of the city called the Mauá, and extends through the heart of the city for a mile to the Monroe Palace. A few years ago this was a tangle of narrow, foul-smelling streets and lanes, which the government was compelled to buy at a large figure. Night and day forces were set at work tearing down the old buildings, removing the débris, constructing the drainage and paving, so that the progress made was remarkably rapid for a tropical country, or for any country or clime. Over three thousand men were kept at work night and day, and four hundred buildings were demolished to carry out the work. In less than two years the change was accomplished, and now this avenue, one hundred and five feet in width, with broad pavements made of mosaic worked into odd designs, a row of brazil trees on each curb, and in the centre, alternating with artistic lamp-posts, has the appearance of one of the famous avenues of Paris. Fine new buildings have been built on each side, many of them of really artistic design and finish. The rounded corner has been used at the street intersections, the building line being on a curve of a considerable radius. This adds a beauty and dignity to the architecture of buildings that is lacking in the cities of the United States.

ONE OF THE BENDS OF THE BEIRA MAR, RIO DE JANEIRO.

The Monroe Palace, which is a reproduction of the Brazilian building at the St. Louis Exposition, and which received a medal for its artistic design, marks the boundary between the two avenues. The building was completed in 1906, and the sessions of the Pan-American conference were held in it during that year, for which it had been specially constructed. It is a beautiful building, and stands in a location where it appears to the very best possible advantage. Here the Beira Mar (around the sea) begins, and it is so named because it runs between the hills and the bay, and follows the outline of the latter. Much of it is made land, and occupies what was at one time the favourite breeding place of the mosquitoes which were formerly the pest of this city. Double roadways in places, of different elevations, small parks, and the ever-varying outline of hill and bay, the intense shades of green of the dense vegetation, and the palms in stately rows and silhouetted against the horizon make this avenue the most beautiful and most fascinating boulevard in the world. I never tired of riding along the Beira Mar, for the angle of vision is constantly changing in its many turns and twists, and every change is only a new vision of beauty and interest. Thus the drive leads out past the Praia da Lapa, the Praia da Russell and the Praia da

Flamengo until it ends in the horseshoe curve of Botafogo, where the exposition of 1908 was held and the buildings of which are yet standing. The Beira Mar is one of the favourite residence districts, and it is lined here and there with beautiful homes. It is easy to go into raptures over such scenes, and dull indeed is the soul that could not be stirred by them.

THE LANDING AT RIO DE JANEIRO.

Among the other streets which have been widened is the Rua Uruguayana, which starts at the custom house and cuts across the city at right angles to the Avenida Central. It is a broad street for a Latin city, but is not so wide as the other. The Avenida do Mangue is a picturesque street, with its quadruple line of stately palms which run its entire length of a mile or more. Rio is the home of the royal palm, and you see them all over the city. The trees are round and smooth and almost as symmetrical as if cut by a sculptor. No avenue of marble columns can equal these furnished by nature. The Canal do Mangue runs through the centre of the Mangue and there are four driveways along it, two on either side of the canal, as it is very broad. Leaving the palms and following the canal, the avenue makes a broad sweep and leads out to the new docks which are being constructed at great expense. Immense warehouses have been built and great cranes erected, but they are not in use, because it is necessary to dredge a channel before the ocean-going vessels of deep draught can reach the docks. Work is progressing, however, and it will not be long until it will no longer be necessary for vessels to anchor out in the open, and for both passengers and freight to be brought ashore either in launches or row boats. Thus will one of the annoyances as well as one of the big items of expense at this port be eliminated. Along the line of warehouses, and parallel with the harbour line, an avenue has been laid out that is more than three hundred feet in width. This gives abundant room for railroad tracks, tram tracks and driveways for both wagons and pleasure vehicles.

There are many pretty little parks scattered over the city, each one of which is a miniature of beauty. The Jardim do Passeio Publico, near the Monroe Palace, is one of these. Its profusion of vegetation is such as can only be seen in a tropical climate, where there is no destroying frost and where a kind nature encourages growth during the entire year. The Praça da Republica is in the very centre of the city, and is the largest park in the city proper. It was the chief theatre of action in the memorable events in which the country was changed from an empire to a republic within the short period of twenty-four hours. Because of this event the name was changed from its former name of Praça d'Acclamacão. There are many statues, in this and all the other parks, of men who have been famous in the country's history. One of the most noted is that of Dom Pedro I in the Praça Tiradentes, which represents him in the act of shouting the watchword "Independence or death," after he received the message from the Portuguese Cortes at Ypiranga, just outside the city of São Paulo. There is also a fine monument to the Duke de Caxais, one of the heroes of the Paraguayan war, in a park which bears his name. Another striking feature of the city is the ancient Carioca Aqueduct, which is a monument of picturesque grandeur where its lofty arches loom up over the comparatively low buildings. It was built more than a century and a half ago, but still remains as solid and substantial as when first built. It is now used by the tramway company as a part of its line which ascends the hill leading up to the Corcovado.

There are many charitable institutions in the city for the care of unfortunates and the amelioration of suffering. There are orphan asylums, free clinics for the treatment of various troubles, an institution maintained by the society formed to combat the plague of tuberculosis, and institutions for the care of the deaf and dumb, blind and insane. The largest hospital in Rio de Janeiro, and perhaps on South American soil, is the Santa Casa de Misericordia, which was founded by the Sisters of Mercy in 1545. The buildings now occupied by this noted institution have been in use for nearly three-quarters of a century, but they have recently been overhauled and remodelled. The buildings are in a classic and beautiful style of architecture, as are most of the public buildings in Brazil. It has accommodation for more than twelve hundred patients. One of the strange and unusual features of this hospital is a revolving wheel made for the reception of unwelcome infants. In this wheel a cradle is so arranged that when an infant is laid on it the wheel turns around, and the little stranger finds a welcome it did not find elsewhere. No questions are asked, no effort is made to find out who placed the infant in the cradle, and the babe is taken care of until it is ready to go forth and work for itself, or has been adopted by some good family. If this institution does nothing else, it takes away the incentive to infanticide which prevails in many places. There is also in the city a Strangers' Hospital, which is mainly supported by the foreign residents of the capital, and it is an institution that has done a great deal of good among those who are expatriated from their homes by the exigencies of business.

The market is always an interesting place to visit in a Latin country, for the life to be seen there is unique. The market scenes in Rio are not so picturesque as in the cities farther inland, but there are still many unique scenes to be witnessed. It is situated just at one side of the Plaza 15th of November, and on the water front, so that the fishing boats can unload direct into the market and the garbage can easily be disposed of. The building is large and commodious, of an indifferent architecture, but well adapted to its purposes. The deepest impression made upon a visit to this place is the decidedly tropical characteristics to be seen everywhere. Tropical fruits, consisting of oranges, bananas, pineapples, mangoes, mammão, etc., are to be seen in great abundance everywhere. The salted meat so commonly used is stacked up like cordwood. It has a strong smell and is very salty, but it is much liked by the common people, and frequently brings a better price than fresh beef. Fat pork is salted in the same way and done up in rolls from which slices are cut off for the customer. This fat is usually used in cooking the beans which form such an important article of food. There are many kinds of strange fish in that department, for the waters along the coast of Brazil are filled with excellent fish. One fish, which is quite large, is very peculiar, because its eyes extend out an inch or more from its head. Then there are little jelly fish in great numbers, and a little creature that looks like a miniature devil-fish which seems to be a favourite article of food. Shrimps and oysters will also be found for sale. Birds of brilliant plumage await the buyers in their cages, while green and purple parrots sit sedately on their perches and fill the air with their rough screeches. Chickens, ducks, geese, turkeys and guinea pigs are found in abundance, and even dogs are caged up awaiting new owners. But the numerous monkeys, from the little marmosettes to the big ones three or four feet high, who sit and blink at you like curious little old men, will probably hold the attention of the northern visitor longer than any other one feature of the market at Rio de Janeiro.

To this market come the hucksters from all parts of the city for their supplies, which they then peddle from door to door. Fish and vegetables are carried in baskets that are hung on the ends of a long pole, which is balanced across the shoulder. A score or more of fowls may be placed in a basket which the peripatetic merchant carries around on his head, while the inmates cackle and crow along the way. The bread merchant carries his stock in trade on his head, in a contrivance which looks more like a baby-crib than anything else. Onions and garlic are carried on strings with the stems woven together with straw. Along the streets one will constantly hear the oddly varying cries of these house-to-house merchants, the flute-like whistles which some of them carry, and the clapping of sticks by others or the strangely penetrating noise of the scissors-grinder, which is made by touching a piece of metal to the grindstone.

From the standpoint of comfort the great and imposing Avenida Central is a failure. The sun beats down unmercifully during the hot days, and it is not half so comfortable as streets like the Ouvidor, Gonçalves Diaz, Quintana and others of the business streets which are so narrow that they are shaded from curb to curb during most of the day, and the sun does not really have a fair chance to get in its work. It is, however, the centre of the street life, and at all times is a study of Brazilian life. There is always a crowd of men in the many cafés, which line this street on either side, and the tables of which are set out over half the broad sidewalk, or more. After eating his noon breakfast, a man never takes his coffee at the same restaurant, but always goes to one of the cafés where he sips a small cup of strong, black coffee, smokes a few cigarettes and gossips with his friends. The Brazilians drink coffee as the German drinks beer—not in such great quantities, but fully as often. In fact they drink so much that it must have got into their complexions. A Brazilian proverb says that good coffee must be as "strong as Satan, as black as ink, as hot as hades and as sweet as love." It is certainly black and strong, is served hot and enough sugar is used to make it very sweet.

One is struck with the vivacity of the groups of men, who talk with their hands, head, face and eyes, as well as with their mouths. Another thing that impressed me was the uncomfortable style of dress, for the average "flumenense" wears a rather heavy suit and derby hat in this hot climate, and would never think of dispensing with his vest under any circumstances. To make up for this one may often see the men carrying fans and briskly fanning themselves. Where these young men, who are clerks in business houses, or hold small-salaried government positions, get the money to spend in these cafés is a mystery to me; for all drinks are exceedingly high-priced, with the exception of coffee, which is uniformly sold for one hundred reis, equal to three cents in our money. In the matter of clothes, however, they are more economical, and they do not dress as well as the ladies whom they delight to watch.

CARIGADORES MOVING A PIANO.

From three to five in the afternoon the Avenida, from the Ouvidor to the Avenida Hotel, is crowded with well-dressed ladies who make these few blocks a sort of promenade. One will see handsomely gowned matrons, demure little maidens, and *senhoritas* who are just beginning to seek the favours of the young men, and this gives them an opportunity to see and be seen. The ladies wear huge Parisian hats and high heels, and are gowned elaborately. Powder, paste, rouge and other cosmetics are much in evidence, even among the younger ones, whose complexions hardly need such aids to freshness. The figures are plump, and those of the matrons have reached a stoutness that must be distressing to them. The men, whose narrow shoulders and thin chests are in striking contrast to the plump figures of the ladies, sit at the street tables of the cafés and watch them as they pass; but they rather like than resent this, for it is the custom of the country, and a long look is a mark of flattery which they appreciate.

In the streets there is a constant movement. Carriages with liveried drivers, high-wheeled carts loaded with freight, curious little Japanese "kiosks," in which walks a vendor of *dulces*, and *carigadores* with loads upon their heads pass along in endless procession. I have seen pianos thus borne upon the heads of four men pass along the Avenida. Other heavy articles of furniture, and large panes of plate glass are carried in the same way. The old-fashioned, two-wheeled tilbury, so common here, whisks along at as lively a rate as the horse can go. Only one passenger dares ride in one of them, or a great commotion will be raised among the other tilbury drivers. The "fon-fon" of the automobile is constantly heard. A line of auto omnibuses is run along this avenue, and then some of the four hundred or more private autos will be in view at any time. Ice is delivered by automobile, for quick delivery is important in a hot climate when the price is three cents a pound. The automobile ambulance is sure to pass along, as it is always on the go, and then there are a number of auto deliveries, police hurry-up wagons, fire trucks, and even a street sprinkler propelled by gasoline.

THE TREASURY BUILDING, RIO DE JANEIRO.

The police are omnipresent, and are to be found everywhere. There are three classes of these guardians of the public peace: the civil, the military and the mounted police. The former are under the prefect, and the military police, who wear a different uniform, are under the authority of the minister of war. The military police may be seen several times a day, marching along in large or small squads with a bugler to announce their coming. The civil police are more numerous but less conspicuous. It is said that there are oftentimes more or less serious conflicts of authority between the two police organizations. The military police department has a number of auto patrol wagons which are frequently seen on the streets. Whenever a call is sent to headquarters a wagon is loaded up with ten or a dozen officers, and is then sent pell-mell through the streets to the point of call, and frequently two wagons thus loaded will appear. Perhaps the occasion of the call is some harmless drunk (although drunkenness is not common), and it seems a joke to see such a formidable force appear upon such an occasion. At night, a policeman may be found upon almost any corner, and, if there is safety in numbers, then Rio de Janeiro is a very secure place in which to live.

Along the Avenida are many fine office buildings belonging to private concerns, some of which cover almost an entire square, and many of which are truly architecturally beautiful structures. Perhaps among the finest of these are the homes of three of the leading newspapers; the *Jornal do Commercio, Jornal do Brazil* and *O Paiz*. The variety of architecture prevents any appearance of monotony. The Caixa de Amortizacão, or treasury building, where the paper and gold money are exchanged and equalized, is a very beautiful building on the corner of the Rua Uruguayana. Near the other end of the Avenida are several fine public buildings. One of these is the new Art Museum, and another the new National Library, neither of which were quite finished at the time of my visit. The Municipal Building is a unique and ornate building, brilliant in colour and adorned with many statues. A number of stately palms which stand near the building give it a very fine setting. The most beautiful and striking building of all, however, is the magnificent Municipal Theatre, which stands in a conspicuous location at a street intersection, and in spacious dimensions, as well as stately appearance, well rivals the far famed Opera House of Paris. It was built by the municipality and cost several millions of dollars, and is said to have a capacity of twenty thousand persons.

THE CITY HALL, RIO DE JANEIRO.

Rio de Janeiro has been transformed. It used to be that the traveller, frightened at the idea of yellow fever, would come here with his ears and brain throbbing from the effects of quinine. He would walk over the city with a smelling bottle under his nose for fear of contagion. Now it is different. Once the home of yellow fever, smallpox and other plagues, this great city has been renovated and overhauled, until now it is as healthful as the average city. The municipal government deserves great credit for the energetic and thorough manner in which this work has been done. Hundreds of miles of underground sewers have supplanted the open gutters of former days, and with the disappearance of the open sewers has vanished the unpleasant odours which formerly pervaded the atmosphere. Low, marshy ground has been filled up. The people were compelled to remove the dirt from the tiles in which moss and fungi had grown, and cement the joints so that there would be nothing to retain dampness. The first floors of all buildings must be made of tile or cement, so that rats can not get into the houses. And then the people scrub and clean, and clean and scrub, in most parts of the city, so that it is a fair rival of a Dutch town. The street cleaning department is alert and active, so that the streets in general are cleaner than the average American city. It is only when one of the heavy rain storms breaks on the city that it is different, and then tons of red sand and mud are washed down from the hills, and the street commissioner has his hands full for a few days to clean up this mud. These tropical rains are veritable downpours, and the amount of water that falls during even a comparatively short rain is almost incredible.

THE "WHITE HOUSE" OF BRAZIL.

The visitor is first inclined to look lightly upon the brilliant and variegated colourings of the houses and other buildings, and think that it is very much overdone. The longer one stays there, however, the more the colouring seems to be in harmony with the tropics. Such brilliant colours and light, airy effects would be entirely out of place in a land where the trees lost their foliage, and snow covered the ground during a part of the year. But here, where the sky is so blue, where the foliage is ever green and where the sun is so bright, even the light blues and greens, the pinks and terra-cotta colourings on the houses finally seem in harmony. Sometimes, under a porch, one will see a landscape painting on the wall of the house, and many of these paintings are well done. The style of architecture is Portuguese and differs from the Spanish style, which always includes a little court, or patio, in the centre. In the Brazilian homes of the better class, a little green yard is maintained in front of the houses, where a few flowers and shrubs are cultivated, and, if large enough, a palm or two will be found. There is no fine grass, however, such as grows in cooler climes, for the grass found is very coarse and is planted stalk by stalk. A high iron fence generally separates the yard from the street. In some of the better homes with large yards, a little pavilion, or lookout, is built near the street, from which the ladies of the family may view the processions and *festas*, which are such a common occurrence here. These take the place of the balconies erected for ladies where the houses are built up to the street line as in the Spanish architecture.

The public buildings are scattered over different sections of the city, but most of them not already enumerated are of rather indifferent architecture. The Casa da Moeda (mint), the Congress and Senate buildings, the Navy and War Departments and the President's Mansion are all in different sections. The latter bears several statues on the roof, and connected with it are some very fine gardens. The National Library contains a valuable collection of more than four hundred thousand books, manuscripts and other important documents. The National Museum is one of the oldest institutions in the capital. Originally intended only as a museum of natural history, it has been extended until now it includes all kinds of collections of scientific interest. It contains a fine collection of specimens of animal and insect life in Brazil, and specimens of the art and handiwork of the aboriginal tribes who still inhabit many sections of the republic.

A splendid system of electric tramways exists under the management of a company composed of American and Canadian capitalists. The routes are rather complicated, and are quite confusing to the visitor at first. The cars are called "bonds," and the origin of the name is rather curious. When the system was first inaugurated the people, who had heard a great deal about American "bonds" in connection with the negotiations, applied that name to the cars when they finally appeared, and the name has clung to them ever since.

The city of Rio de Janeiro and its environs constitute the Federal District, which is similar to the District of Columbia. The municipal organization is controlled by the national government, but the people are not disfranchised as in our own capital. The inhabitants of the district elect three senators and ten deputies to the National Congress, and also a city council of ten members which meets in session twice each year. The chief executive is the Prefect, who is appointed by the President and holds office for five years, unless previously removed. Under him are several boards, through which the several departments of public work are transacted.

In 1908 there was held in Rio an exposition in celebration of the centennial of the opening of that port, and the other Brazilian ports to the commerce of the world. The federal government appropriated a million dollars for its palace and exhibit, and nearly all of the states erected buildings, and appropriated a goodly sum toward the expenses. The United States and Portugal were the only two foreign nations invited to take a part in the exposition. The location was a most beautiful one at the extreme end of the Beira Mar, and almost under the shadow of old Sugar Loaf and Corcovado. A number of the buildings erected were of a permanent character, and these, as well as many of the state buildings, still stand.

In striking contrast to the Rio of to-day was that of a century ago, when foreign nations were first given the privilege of trading there. The following extracts are made from "Notices of Brazil," published in 1831 by an English writer:

"When the country was opened to the enterprise of foreigners, it was not at all surprising that the City of Rio and its commerce should have increased with an unexampled rapidity. Such was the avidity of speculation in England, that everything was sent to Brazil without the smallest regard to its fitness or adaptation to the climate, or the wants of the people who were to purchase them. The shops were ransacked and swept; and the consideration was not what should be sent, but how soon could it arrive. In this way, when the multitude of cases were opened at the custom-house, I have been told, the Brazilians could not contain their astonishment and mirth at the incongruous things they saw displayed before them; implements useful only to Canadians and Greenlanders, and comforts and conveniences fit only for polar latitudes, were cased up and sent in abundance to regions between the tropics.

"Among this ingenious selection was a large supply of warm blankets, warming-pans to heat them, and, to complete the climax of absurdity, skates to enable the Brazilians to enjoy wholesome exercise on the ice, in a region where a particle of frost or a flake of snow was never seen. However ridiculous or wasteful this may seem, these incongruous articles were not lost in a new country, where necessity and ingenuity could apply things to a use for which they were never intended by the sage exporters. Even the apparently hopeless and inconvertible skate was turned to a useful purpose. Then, as well as now, there was nothing in the country so scarce as wrought iron for shoeing mules and horses; and though "ferradors," or smiths, are to be met at every rancho, "ferraduras," or shoes, are seldom to be had. When the people, therefore, found they could not use these contrivances on their own, they applied them to their horses' feet; and many an animal has actually travelled on English skates from Rio to Villa Rica.

"The bustle and activity of the place give a high idea of the commerce of Rio. A multitude of negroes are constantly employed, who labour without intermission the whole day in removing packages of different kinds. They are generally lying open, either to be, or after having been examined; and it presents really a curious and interesting spectacle to pass along the courts and warerooms, through manufactures of every kind, and from all parts of the globe.

"Having waded through these, I mounted upstairs, and I saw a multitude of persons hard at work, as if it had been a large factory. These were the stampers: every article, even to a single pair of gloves, stockings or shoes, when the duty is paid, must be distinguished by this stamp. Three or four hundred persons were engaged in this work. One ran the thread through the corner of the stockings or shoes; another looped it to a little perforated pellet of lead; and a third pressed it flat by striking on it a stamp of the Imperial Arms. Any article, however minute, that has not this attachment to it, is liable to be seized as contraband. The process of stamping every article, however, is so tedious and troublesome that it is found to impede business very much, and the fees on the leaden stamp come to twice as much as the duty on the goods in the cost of pieces of tape and other smaller things."

CHAPTER IV
AROUND AND ABOUT THE BAY

There are many villages large and small, around the Bay of Rio de Janeiro, but few of them are worth the visiting. Nictheroy, however, a twenty minutes' ride across the bay, is an exception, for the ride is pleasant and this city is the capital of the state of Rio de Janeiro. The national capital is situated in a Federal District very similar to the District of Columbia. Ferries run every few minutes, and the trip is a pleasant diversion. The city contains some thirty thousand or more inhabitants, but there is nothing grand or distinctive about it. It has several public squares after the usual fashion, the streets are fairly broad but badly paved, and some of the public buildings are quite respectable. There is a good system of street railways, and a trip can be made out to the rather picturesque suburb of Sacco do San Francisco, or Itajahý, which is also on the shores of the bay. Perhaps the principal reason that takes travellers there is to say that they have been in one of the state capitals, for it is too near the larger and far more attractive city to have much charm when compared with the other. There is a good beach, and it is possible that at some time, perhaps "to-morrow," a thriving resort may be built up on that side of the blue bay of Rio de Janeiro.

During the empire, because of the many and almost constant scourges of yellow fever, the diplomatic corps became solicitous about their own health and sought a more healthful residence. Receiving the consent of their various governments, and the approval of the Emperor, a new diplomatic residence was established at Petropolis, a two hours' journey from the capital. This is the only instance known to me where the diplomatic representatives live elsewhere than in the capital of the country to which they are accredited.

The journey to this diplomatic centre is at the present time a combined rail and steamer journey, although within a very short time, and perhaps by the time this work appears, it will be possible to make the journey by rail in a little more than half the time now necessary. If one has the time, however, the combination journey is preferable, because it affords a delightful journey across the blue waters of the bay, past the Fiscal Island with its imposing edifice, near a number of other islands to the Mauá landing where a connection is made with the oldest railway in the republic. The first rails of this line, which is now a part of the Leopoldina System, were laid more than a half century ago. Almost immediately after entering the train the ascent begins, for it is a climb of nearly a thousand metres to this other capital of the country. As the train ascends many new and varying glimpses are caught of the island-studded bay, and even of the city of Rio many miles away, with Corcovado and Tijuca in the background. The cloud effects vary with almost every trip. At times almost the entire bay is seen, and then again, only fleeting glimpses are visible, as you seem to be looking down upon a bed of billowy clouds. When the steepest part of the road is reached the train is divided into small sections, and the upward ascent is aided by the cog system, although very powerful locomotives are used.

A maximum grade of fifteen per cent. is reached in one or two places, which is a very steep climb indeed, and you feel like holding yourself in your seat. Narrow valleys, or rather passes, are traversed and there is some cultivation, but the most of the way is rather a mass of trailing vines and great, branching ferns. Blossoming vines and trees add beauty to the scene, and immense trees loaded with orchids look down upon you in a tantalizing way; detached rocks weighing thousands of tons are poised on the edge of cliffs, and show the glacial effects in these passes. Sometimes the brown and grim rocks rise above you like a mighty wall a thousand or more feet high, as if nature had prepared a natural fort or a gigantic toboggan slide ready for use. The little mountain streams had become swift torrents, when I passed over this road, from the effects of a severe storm that had just broken on these hills. The air becomes much cooler as the elevation increases. At last the Alta da Serra, the top of the mountain, is reached, and from there it is an easy ride down to Petropolis nestling between lofty peaks.

Being the headquarters of a score or more representatives of the world's powers, Petropolis is an important city. Furthermore, during the hottest season, it is the fashionable summer resort of Brazilian society, and the wealth and gayety of the capital is transferred to this city. From a small agricultural settlement it has grown into a social centre, an educational centre and the site of a number of cotton mills, which are located here because of the abundant water power. The scenery about Petropolis is beautiful, and affords a number of fine drives and horseback jaunts, which are the favourite recreation of the diplomats. It is a combination of the temperate and tropical zones. Your hothouse plants all grow out-of-doors. Rhododendrons are as large as wheat shocks, and the azaleas are so large they do not look natural. Palms are omnipresent, and the orange with its golden fruit ornaments almost every yard.

The last Emperor, Dom Pedro II., had a beautiful home here which is now used as a young ladies' seminary. There are also a number of other good schools, among which is a school for girls under the auspices of the Methodist Episcopal Church South. It is situated on the top of a hill above the city. The rooms have lofty ceilings eighteen feet high, its bathroom is as large as the average living-room, and in every way it resembles the palace which it once was, rather than a school building. Yet as one looks around at the American desks, the blackboards, maps, etc., on the walls, the school stamp is readily seen.

The social season lasts from December to May, the Brazilian summer, and during that time the social life is gay, but it is rather dull the rest of the year. The President, and most of his ministers, spend these months here, and Petropolis thus becomes the summer capital. There are many fine homes of Brazilian families, and some of the diplomatic representatives occupy showy quarters. The home of the American Ambassador is a delightful and charming place. The air is remarkably cool, especially in the evening, even when Rio is sweltering. It is quite likely that the official residences of the diplomats will be changed to Rio at some time in the future, since the sanitary conditions have been so improved, and yellow fever is no longer found there, except in an occasional sporadic case such as might occur at some of our own Gulf ports.

CLUSTERS OF BAMBOOS IN THE JARDIM BOTANICO.

There are many notable botanical gardens in the world, but there is only one, in the general consensus of opinion, which is superior to that of Rio de Janeiro, and it is in Buitenzorg, Java. To the northern traveller every park in Rio is a sort of botanical garden, because of the many and new varieties of plants, but a visit to the famous Jardim Botanico, which is reached by one of the "bonds" that start from the Avenida Hotel, is a revelation. The route leads out through a number of narrow streets. At one place a branch line runs to Leme by a tunnel through one of the hills, where a pretty stretch of beach may be seen. It has become quite a favourite resort as well as residence place, and is worth a visit.

Continuing the journey the car passes by a small lake, called Lago Ridrigo de Freitas, which is a fresh water lake, although separated from the sea by only a narrow stretch of land. There are some interesting old country-houses and modern villas, and a number of cotton factories with their rows of workingmen's houses built on the community plan. Many fine glimpses of Tijuca, the Two Brothers and Corcovado are obtained along the way. At last the avenue of palms grows nearer, the car stops before a gateway of recent construction, and the famous gardens have been reached.

Before one's vision extends a magnificent avenue of lofty royal palms of even height. This avenue, composed of one hundred and fifty palms, set at equal distances apart, and making a green arch almost a hundred feet above ground, makes an imposing picture like a great colonnade, with their white trunks. As you look up the avenue you see two gigantic walls of gray wood, solidly roofed by huge green tufts. It is a living arborescent gallery, enclosing a path about twenty feet wide with a neatly gravelled walk. About half-way across is a fountain in the centre of the avenue, and here is another avenue of palms which runs at right angles to the other, but this avenue is far less imposing than the one just described. The contrast between the lofty palms and some of the pygmy shrubs and flowers is most striking. In one part of the gardens still stands a single palm, a tall, slender shaft one hundred and twenty-five feet in height, which is called the "mother of all the palms." It was planted in 1808, the year of the foundation of this garden, with elaborate ceremony by the Portuguese regent, and from the seeds of this palm have been grown all the other royal palms in this garden, so it is said. A tablet has been placed on this palm bearing a statement of this fact.

Another feature which is most interesting is the profusion of bamboos, which are found in dense clusters, and also in shady avenues, where the tops are so intertwined that it is impossible for the sun to penetrate through. One begins to appreciate the beauties of the graceful bamboo when seen under such advantageous conditions. Sometimes an avenue is lined for some distance with similar trees, then with others; sometimes with one species on one side of the walk and an entirely different species on the other side; again they are in clumps all alike or all different, an endless variety in grouping. Fine specimens of the rubber trees are to be seen, and one can get a good idea of this tree which yields such a valuable article of commerce to the world of to-day. The clove, nutmeg, cinnamon and other spice-bearing trees, which are many decades old, may be seen, as well as specimens of the tea plant. The "cow tree," which secretes a fluid that resembles milk, and a tree which, upon being tapped, pours forth a stream of pure, cold water may both be found.

It will not be necessary for one to travel up the Amazon to see the vegetation that grows there, for specimens of almost every species may be found here. Monster trees from the Amazon country which overtop even the lofty royal palms, and reach a height of from one hundred and fifty to two hundred feet, grow here luxuriantly. Trees with great buttresses, which look like strained muscles, and others, with gigantic vines clinging to them, which are slowly sapping the life out of the friendly tree, grow here, just as they do in the primeval forests. Parasites of every kind may be seen on the trunks, and in the angles formed by the limbs. Some of the trees are almost covered with these parasitic growths. Orchids, which would be almost priceless in the markets of New York, are found blooming here amidst the wild tangle of vines. Specimens of the gigantic lily, called the Victoria Regis, a native of Brazil, and whose leaves measure from ten to twenty feet in diameter, grow in the waters of this same garden. There are also little glimpses of almost virgin forest, that may be seen in the two thousand acres of this treasure-house of botanical specimens. The many shades of green are varied by the colours of the poincetta and other flowers, and in and through all flit birds of many hues, swift flying humming birds and monstrous butterflies. The researches which have been made by the various learned directors of these botanical gardens have proven of inestimable value to the scientific world.

One soon discovers that Rio has more than the seven hills which were boasted by Rome, for there are three times that number that look down upon the bay. A number of these rounded knolls are within the borders of the city itself, and the narrow, winding streets crawl up to the very summit. Others are surmounted by a few houses, while the sides of the hills simply display their red slope to the city. But it is to the suburbs that one must go for the finest views of the city and surrounding country. One of the favourite trips is to Tijuca, the summit of which is almost reached by an electric line, and many of the wealthier people have their summer or all-the-year-round homes on its slopes. As the road climbs up to the summit, many beautiful views are obtained of the scenery surrounding Rio. It is a view of peaks, and valleys and ocean, for very little of the city is visible. The road passes through dense forests, so that one is constantly sheltered from the fierce sun.

Sylvan pathways are flanked with beautiful plants, shrubs and flowers. Leaping cascades are set in veritable flower gardens, and natural labyrinths and grottos abound. The highest point is nearly fourteen hundred feet above sea level. This route is now a favourite automobile drive also, but is not safe to make after heavy rains because of the narrow roadway in many places.

It is, however, to Corcovado that one goes for a magnificent view of Rio and the bay of the same name. This famous hunchback mountain almost overshadows the city and the climb up affords views of dazzling magnificence. It is a great granite cone, precipitous on all sides save one, and an electric line, which follows this slope, now takes the traveller almost to the very summit. Leaving the station in the city, the road first runs over the old and well-preserved Carioca Aqueduct where, for a few blocks, the car runs along high above the red-tiled roofs of the capital city. Then it begins the climb up along the side of the mountain. Now one obtains a view of the bay, and again one looks out over the city to the Serra da Mar mountains in the distance; again it is Tijuca, or the peak of Tingue, that dominates the horizon. The abandoned aqueduct follows the bends of the road and has been broken in many places, for new water pipes now carry the water supply from the original source. An old and famous convent, Santa Theresa, is seen, where husbands used to place their wives for safekeeping when departing on a military expedition. Past hotels, villages and showy private homes the road winds and twists. Finally the line changes to the rack system, as the grade becomes more steep, and at last, after a climb for a few minutes up steps hewed out of the solid rock, the little pavilion is reached that crowns the mountain's summit. Here beautiful views meet the gaze of the traveller in every direction; mountains on one side, the sea and beautiful bay on the other. On a clear day a panorama of fifty square miles may be seen with the unaided eye. Sheer precipices of more or less bare rock extend down for a distance of fifteen hundred feet or more. A stone merely dropped over the crowning walls would descend to the plains below. It is to the bay that one will turn with most interest. There, in the distance, is the seemingly narrow channel through which all boats must pass on their way to the city. Then nearer to the city is the famous Sugar Loaf, with its curious outline. The blue waters of the bay studded with numerous small islands, the curved shores, the white streaks which mark the cities, and the broad white line, which indicates the Avenida Central and the Beira Mar, acquire a new meaning, and become photographed upon one's memory in indelible colours; it is then one fully realizes that he is gazing upon one of the most beautiful panoramas that nature has prepared for the delectation of mankind.

CHAPTER V
MINAS GERAES AND MINING

There is another route to Bello Horizonte, the capital of the state of Minas Geraes, but I chose the one through Petropolis, because I was to have the pleasure of the company of the American Embassador. Petropolis was the one time capital of the state of Rio de Janeiro. There are other cities in the state of Rio besides Petropolis. Among these are Therezopolis, which occupies a magnificent site on a commanding hill that gives a fine view of the surrounding country, and Nova Friburgo, the oldest immigrant settlement in Brazil. This city was established almost a century ago by a number of Swiss colonists, and is reached by another railway of almost an equal ascent with the route to Petropolis, heretofore described. This little colony has grown into a prosperous settlement and preserves many of the characteristics of the race which founded it.

Boarding the semi-weekly express train at Petropolis, which is here termed *"grande velocidade,"* we were soon winding around the hills and through the narrow passes threaded by the river. Occasionally little primitive villages and a few unimportant adobe towns picturesquely grouped along the banks of the stream were passed. The scenery is beautiful as pass after pass unfolds itself on the journey down to lower altitudes. One is impressed by the extent of mountainous territory which is encountered by the traveller all over the republic, with the exception of the country traversed by the mighty Amazon and its tributaries. It is a constant surprise to see the vast amount of soil in Brazil that is actually without development. Mile after mile of this land, which is within a comparatively short distance of the capital, had the appearance of never having been occupied by settlers, or ever having been disturbed by agriculturists. Although broken it could well be adapted to the raising of stock, at least for sheep and goats, for these animals would find sustenance. It seemed to me that cattle could be raised profitably also, since it would not be necessary to feed them, as pasture will grow all the year round.

AN OX TEAM OF MINAS GERAES.

The few natives who did live in the little mud-brick huts, with thatch roofs, that cling to the side of the hills eked out a very poor existence, if one judged by the appearance of everything around their homes. A few chickens and pigs with plenty of dogs, perhaps a mule and a cow, constituted the only stock that one could see. A little patch of corn, a banana stalk or two, and perhaps a patch of mandioca root, seemed to be the only attempt at agriculture of the improvident negro or poor whites who dwell on these beautiful hills. The houses contain only the very crudest of furniture with rude beds and the very simplest of culinary outfit. Nature is perhaps too bountiful, and man depends upon that bounty rather than his own exertions.

The mandioca is a small shrub with a tuberous root that grows in nearly every part of Brazil. It grows to the enormous size of fifteen and twenty pounds, and somewhat resembles an enormous radish or sugar beet. In its natural state it contains a very poisonous juice which must be eliminated before the real substance can be used for food. It is first pressed and then washed, and the water must be thrown away for it is poisonous. The root is then ground into a meal which is very rich in starch. One large root will sometimes produce as much as two gallons of this prepared meal. After being crushed the meal is at once roasted, or otherwise it will turn sour and be spoiled. Tapioca is one of the products of this tropical tuber. The utilization of this root was first discovered by the Indians, who found a method of getting rid of the poisonous qualities. To-day, the mandioca, or farina, flour is one of the principal articles of food in Brazil, not only among the poorer classes but also with the well-to-do. Many of the articles served on the hotel tables are thickened with the mandioca meal. This, with rice and beans, furnishes the almost exclusive food of the poor. On the railway trains one will see that this meal comprises one of the chief articles of the lunches which have been brought by one's fellow passengers.

It is perhaps wrong to think only of the practical in the midst of scenes of natural beauty, but as our train whirled along with its *grande velocidade*, past rapids which could be converted into incalculable power for the manufacturing so essential in the world, I could not refrain from thinking what fine power was here going to waste. A little of it is utilized in generating electricity for the cities of Nictheroy and Petropolis, and there are a few cotton mills run by the water power of this stream. Not one unit of the available power is utilized, however, although in this land of expensive fuel there is a great call for electric power and current. At last the Parahyba River, a still finer stream of water, is reached and the railroad follows up this stream. At Entre Rios (which means "between the rivers") a change is made from the Leopoldina Railway to the Central, which is a government line. After a couple of hours the train reaches Juiz de Fora, which is the largest town in the state of Minas Geraes. In 1867 Juiz de Fora was described by a writer as a town with "a single dusty or muddy street, or rather road, across which palms are planted in pairs."

At the present time this city contains a population of perhaps twenty-five or thirty thousand people. It is in a region of great productiveness, and in a mild and semi-tropical climate. The surrounding hilly country forms a rich and extensive coffee district, and is also very favourable to the growth of corn and beans, as well as other products. Cattle raising is also an important industry. It is a comparatively modern town, and its streets are laid out much wider than the older towns. There are several colleges here, and the public schools are unusually good, so that the number of educated persons is exceeded by few places in the entire republic. Several small manufacturing industries have been established to make use of the rapids in the Parahyba River which flows through the city.

About a ten hours' journey in a northerly direction from Juiz de Fora lies Bello Horizonte, the new capital of the state of Minas Geraes. After leaving Juiz de Fora the railroad climbs the higher altitudes, and it is not long until the coffee region is left behind. The atmosphere becomes cooler and more exhilarating as the altitude increases. Like most of the cities Bello Horizonte is built in a valley surrounded by hills, with a river running through it. It is a city made to order, for the site was selected only sixteen years ago. At that time there was scarcely a habitation on the chosen site, but the location seemed to please the government and so it was decided to erect a city to be used as a capital. Like La Plata, in Argentina, it is a city built after an architect's designs, and, because of the elaborate plans made for it, was given the name *bello*," which signifies beautiful. It has been likened by the enthusiastic Brazilians to our own city of Washington, because of its broad avenues and many plazas, and the modern style of its buildings. The principal avenue, Affonso Penna, named after the late President, who founded this city while he was President of the state, is one hundred and fifty feet broad, and has a triple row of shade trees its entire length. The public buildings are attractive because of their newness, and are a radical departure from most of the public buildings that one may see in Brazil. A magnificent palace for the executive has been erected, and a number of buildings for the legislature and other branches of the government. The city is well lighted and is altogether a bright and cheery place.

The state of Minas Geraes is one of the largest and most important states in Brazil. It is larger than France and contains a population of more than four millions of people. It derives its names from its mineral wealth, for Minas Geraes signifies general mines. It has within its borders many mines, and possesses the oldest gold mine in the country. There are many small towns but no large cities, so that most of the population dwell in small villages. Much of this state, like many of the others, is still undeveloped, and railroads have not yet penetrated large sections of it.

This state has the honour of having struck the first blow for freedom from the oppressive rule of Portugal. Joachim José de Silva Xavier is the traditional hero of this event in Brazil. This patriot was a travelling dentist and, because of his occupation, was nicknamed Tiradentes, which means "to draw teeth." He belonged to a club of men who had banded together for patriotic purposes. Spurred on by the success of the American revolution, and angered by the attempt of the mother country to impose iniquitous taxes upon the colony, these men met in secret for many months. Tiradentes in his trips around the country preached his revolutionary doctrine, and many new adherents were added to their cause. The wandering dentist was probably not the originator of the various schemes of this body of dreamers, for far abler men than he were among them, but he probably did more to spread the doctrine than any of the others. At length, in 1789, before their plans were fully matured, the plot was discovered, and the leaders were arrested in Ouro Preto, at that time the capital, and thrust into prison in that city. They were imprisoned in dark and damp cells for many months, pending the trial and decision of the matter.

Each one of the conspirators was finally condemned to death, but all escaped this extreme penalty through influential connections, except the unfortunate Tiradentes. He was made the scapegoat of the whole affair, and was executed in the public square of Ouro Preto, on the 21st of April, 1792. His body was quartered and the head exposed in that city. The right arm and leg, and also the left arm and leg, were each sent to different cities, there to be exposed publicly as a warning to other possible conspirators. His house was torn down and the ground salted to purify it; and it was ordered that no building ever again be constructed on that tainted soil. His property was confiscated; his family and their descendants were declared "infamous" and disgraced, even to the third generation. To-day, the name of Tiradentes is honoured all over Brazil, monuments have been erected to him and streets named after him in many cities. In the principal plaza of Ouro Preto is a marble column, upon which stands a statue of the martyred "tooth-puller." The pedestal of this monument is the original stone on which he was exposed in a pillory and publicly scourged, on the very spot on which now stands his splendid monument. Many of the places connected with this conspiracy are preserved; and even the spot on which stood the house of Tiradentes, which was destroyed by order of the government, is sacredly preserved and guarded for the patriotic lessons which it teaches.

A branch of the Central Railroad runs from the main line back among the hills to this city of Ouro Preto, the "black gold." It lies in the hollow of a narrow valley and is completely surrounded by high, rock-capped hills. All about the hills are the rough, red and gray, yellow and brown holes made by the old miners, which have been enlarged and washed by the rains. The roughly paved streets ascending and descending the hills are narrow, crooked and irregular. Carts and carriages are of little use, and the freight is generally carried on the backs of pack mules. One can see building timbers, stones, flour and water thus carried through the streets of Ouro Preto on almost any day.

Although gold mining in Brazil never reached the proportions it did in Mexico and Peru, it was no inconsiderable factor in the early development of the country. As early as the middle of the sixteenth century, parties of intrepid pioneers had penetrated several hundred miles into the interior. They found auriferous ground in some of the streams in what is now the state of Minas Geraes. As soon as the news reached the settlements other parties of explorers followed, and the tablelands, mountains and streams of this district were overrun from São Paulo to the south and from Bahia on the east. One can not help but admire the rugged courage of these sturdy prospectors, who set out into the tractless forests and moorlands in search of the yellow metal. They bridged rivers, enslaved the Indians and dotted the province with little settlements. It was not long until a small but steady stream of gold was trickling across the sea to Portugal. The crown exacted a tax of twenty per cent. on the entire output, and this naturally led to a great deal of smuggling.

Because of this surreptitious mining it is impossible to give the entire output of the gold mines of this province. Official records, however, show that between the years 1700 and 1820, no less than thirty million ounces having a value of more than $500,000,000 were produced. Legends of the fabulous production of certain mines are recounted, and a few mines were worked for more than a century.

Because of the crude methods in use, and the difficulty of working them at great depths, many of the mines were abandoned before they were really exhausted. One of the principal mines now worked is the Morro Velho, which was operated in a desultory way for a long time by the colonial settlers. In 1818 it was pronounced exhausted. A few years later this mine was reopened and has been worked by an English company ever since, and is still producing a profitable output. It has now reached a great depth. Gold is found nearly all over the state of Minas, although the production to-day is not so great as in the earlier days. A great deal of it is low grade ore, which can be worked profitably only with the latest improved machinery, so that not only the cost of operation can be reduced to a minimum but the greatest percentage of the gold and silver may be extracted from the gravel and quartz.

Many other minerals are found in this state, but few of them are worked. There are a number of iron outcrops reported which are said to be composed of almost pure ore. Copper has been found in Minas, as well as in several other states, although little exploitation has been done, and platinum is also mined. Brazil contains the largest mines of manganese ore that have yet been discovered. This metal promises to be of more value in the future. Monazite, an essential element in the manufacture of mantles for incandescent gas lights, is mined in large quantities and shipped to Europe.

Many precious stones are found in Brazil. Among them are amethysts, tourmalines, aquamarines, topaz—and, lastly, the diamond. India was the original source of diamonds. In 1728, almost two centuries ago, these precious stones were first discovered in Brazil. For a century and a half Brazil held the absolute supremacy in the production of diamonds, until the discovery of the South African fields transferred the centre of the diamond industry to that region. Although the number of diamonds of Brazil to-day is far less than those of South Africa, it is said by experts that the Brazilian diamonds have a far larger proportion of what are classed as the "first water," those which have a tinge of bluish steel in them, than any other country, and the diamonds of that country bring the very highest market price.

The centre of the diamond industry in Brazil is at Diamantina, in the state of Minas Geraes, although these precious stones are also found in the states of Motto Grosso, Bahia, Goyaz, and Paraná. Heretofore the methods of mining diamonds in Brazil have been of the very crudest sort, the same that have been used almost from the time of the first discovery. Just recently American capital has purchased the leading mines, and modern dredging machinery has been installed, as well as machinery for the separation of the gravel products from the diamonds. These machines are run by water power generated from the streams along which the diamonds are found. This will revolutionize the diamond industry in Brazil, and the possibilities are that the production of diamonds in that country will be greatly increased.

There is, and has always been, a fascination about the diamond. Not only is it unrivalled for lustre, brilliancy and fire, but it is so hard that no known substance can cut it or make the slightest indentation save, another diamond. The popular saying that it takes a diamond to cut a diamond is literally true. Furthermore, it is composed of pure carbon, and is thus related to two of the commonest of substances, coal and graphite. The appearance of the diamond when first picked up is very different from its appearance after the skillful cutter and polisher have done their work, for it is very dull and the non-expert would probably not recognize it.

The discovery of the diamonds in Brazil was by accident. In searching for gold and silver some singular stones, supposed to be pebbles, were discovered. The negro labourers were attracted by their uncommon qualities and geometric forms, and showed them to their masters. In the card games which were popular in the mining camps these pebbles had been used for counters. At length, an officer, who had been in India, and had seen the diamonds of that country, suspicioned their real nature. Upon a comparison of the weight with other pebbles he found a great difference. As a result some were sent to Lisbon to be examined, from whence they were forwarded to Holland, and the Hollanders pronounced them to be real diamonds. It has been estimated that during the one hundred and eighty-one years since the discovery of diamonds, Brazil has produced two and one-half metric tons of these valuable stones, or twelve million carats. The value of the production each year amounts to about one million dollars of actual value. This is small in comparison with the mines of South Africa, but no such force or vitality has been expended in the mining. And yet the production is much simpler. The diamantiferous fields of South Africa have required the most expensive machinery, and every device that human ingenuity could devise for the successful extraction of the diamonds. In Brazil, so far as discovered, the diamond deposits are all alluvial and are found on the surface, and in or along the beds of rivers. Hence no deep mining is necessary as in Africa. These river gravels also contain a considerable amount of gold, which helps to pay the cost of dredging. The primitive processes in use are very similar to those in use in placer gold washing. The gravel is dug out and placed in small wooden bowls. The miners then proceed to a convenient place on the stream and laboriously wash out their material, gradually getting rid of the particles not wanted. Sometimes a pit is excavated, and a part of the stream diverted into it for the washing process.

Although no diamonds have been found in Brazil as large as some of the extraordinary gems that have been unearthed in the Kimberly mines, some beautiful and large stones have been discovered. One of these, called the "Regent of Portugal," weighed two hundred and fifteen carats, and has been estimated to be worth more than a million dollars. It is now numbered among the French state jewels. Another was the "Star of the South," which was found by a negress who was at work in the mines near Diamantina. This diamond weighed in the rough two hundred and fifty-four and one-half carats, but when cut was reduced to one hundred and twenty-five carats. It is a fine stone of first quality. A large one was discovered in 1908 which was one and one-third inches long and three-quarters of an inch in width, which would make it of extraordinary size.

The discovery of the Braganza diamond is an interesting story. This was in 1791. Three men who had been convicted of capital offences were sent out into exile among the Indians and wild beasts. As they were forbidden to enter any city, or hold any communication with the world, they searched for treasure. While washing for gold in the Abaite River, they were attracted by the gleam of a curious stone. As diamond washing was prohibited they took the stone to a priest. He ventured to lead them to the governor, and the diamond was presented to him. At the request of the priest the three men were pardoned, but the government retained the gem.

The black diamonds, called "carbonados," are found in greater quantities in Brazil than in any other country. These are used solely for commercial purposes in making points for drills. They are as hard as the other diamonds, but lack the transparency and brilliancy of the white stones. The "carbonados" are found in much larger sizes than the others, one of three thousand and seventy-eight carats having been discovered. These stones have a considerable value and are worth from $25 to $75 per carat, the price depending upon the demand and supply. Nothing has ever been discovered that is so good for drilling hard rocks as the diamond drills made from these "carbonados," and they have been successfully used in drilling many railroad tunnels.

CHAPTER VI
A PROGRESSIVE STATE

It is a distance of three hundred miles from Rio to São Paulo, the second city in the republic, and the ride is very interesting, especially so for the first two or three hours. This time is taken by the railway line to climb over the ridge of mountains, which everywhere pass close to the shore. For some time after leaving the Central station in Rio, the train passes through the city and suburban towns, over which a good and frequent suburban service is run. Then a strip of rather low land gives the traveller a fairly good view of a Brazilian forest of small trees and undergrowth, matted together with parasites, and forming an almost compact mass of green in which many orchids may be seen. Fairly well cultivated fields are passed at intervals until the ascent begins at Belem, from which time there is very little cultivation. Some grand glimpses of mountain scenery are revealed as the train turns around bends and emerges from one or another of the numerous tunnels along the line. Mountains, hills and valleys, flowing streams and cascades, mingle in a panorama of wonderful beauty. At Barra do Pirahy the São Paulo road branches off from the line to Bello Horizonte, and gradually descends to lower levels.

Much of the land, as the slopes become less steep, has been cultivated in the past with coffee, but it is now abandoned. Dead, or nearly dead, coffee trees are still standing amidst the wild growth that has sprung up since the land was abandoned. This part of Minas Geraes was at one time regarded as one of the richest coffee sections in Brazil, and would be valuable land even to-day were it not for the improvident and wasteful methods of the average planter. The trees were planted too thick, and no effort made to place back in the soil any of the elements taken out. It was considered cheaper to buy virgin soil in a new location than to do anything to build up the land already owned. The same thing is seen in other parts of Minas Geraes and the state of Rio de Janeiro, the latter being the state in which was originally grown the famous "Rio" coffee.

The road follows the Parahyba River most of the way, sometimes on one bank and again on the other. The valleys become broader, although occasionally a cut is made through an interesting ridge. The towns are more numerous and larger during the last hundred miles. The Italian element grows more pronounced, and many Italians may be seen at the stations and on the trains. Ox teams drawing clumsy carts seem to be the principal conveyances for freight, and two-wheeled carriages of an antiquated type, which must have been the originals of the London hansom cabs, convey the passengers. At one station an old style automobile was sandwiched in between these two classes of vehicles, and it seemed strangely out of place, except that the automobile was as antiquated for that class of conveyances as the others were in their line.

Immense ant hills dot the landscape in many places. These hills are oftentimes from three to four or five feet in height, and look strangely like old-fashioned bee hives with their rounded tops. The red dust sifts in through the car windows in clouds. As the windows must be kept closed on this account, one is given a turkish bath under very disadvantageous circumstances. Furthermore, no matter how hot it is, the sweltering traveller is not permitted to remove his coat, as that is a breach of etiquette not allowed here. I tried it and was immediately requested very politely to put it on. You may expectorate on the floor as much as you like, but to remove your coat—"No, Senhor; it is against the rules of the company."

The dust is caused by the red clay which is used as a ballast here because it is found all along the line, and is cheaper than stone. A few coffee fields are passed, and then we enter a valley many miles broad, and one has his first glimpse of really level land in Brazil. At length, after eleven hours' ride, the train rolls into the Norte station of the City of São Paulo, and the *carigadores* begin their struggle for your luggage. Then, after being released from their clutches, you are turned over to the tender mercies of the cabman, and the traveller welcomes the comfort of a bath in his hotel to get rid of the dust of travel.

The city of São (pronounced Sah-o, with a nasal sound after the a) Paulo is the second city in the republic in population and commercial importance. It is situated on a plain with low hills upon the entire horizon. Its population is in the neighbourhood of three hundred and fifty thousand. Although little coffee is produced within fifty miles of São Paulo, yet it is the centre of that trade, and the great increase in the production has caused the wonderful growth of this city. It is more like an American city than any of the other Brazilian towns, because, in whatever direction one looks, the high smoke-stacks of some of the many factories may be seen. The suburbs are many and new, and everywhere are signs of building activity and the construction of public improvements. The growth of the city has really been marvellous. Twenty years ago São Paulo was a comparatively unimportant city of twenty-five thousand people. Now it has grown and broadened out until it covers a wide territory. Real estate values have increased until to-day real estate on Rua São Bento, or Rua Quinze de Novembro (15th of November), is almost as high as on the principal streets in similar towns of the United States. It has become the distributing and manufacturing centre for this, the most progressive state in the republic. The temperature of São Paulo may have something to do with the energetic character of the people. Although the latitude is not much different from Rio, its altitude of more than 2,000 feet renders the climate very agreeable. I was there in the middle of their summer, and, although the days were quite warm, the nights were delightfully cool, and blankets were very comfortable on one's bed.

RUA DIREITA, SÃO PAULO.

The business centre of the city is a triangle composed of the two streets above mentioned, and the Rua Direita, the straight street. Around this triangle in the afternoons the ladies walk on their shopping tours; in the evening it is the promenade, and all the people who are down town at night may be seen somewhere on that route. São Paulo is not a typical Brazilian town, for it has outgrown many of those characteristics to be seen in the towns which are more peculiarly Portuguese. There is a large foreign element, and their influence is notable in every part of the city, and even in the life of the Paulistas themselves. A great deal of the exclusiveness of the family life has disappeared, and the young women of the city may be seen out upon the street on a shopping tour, or performing an errand, unaccompanied by the duenna, which would be unknown in more conservative Rio. There are perhaps one hundred thousand Italians in the city, and added to these are several thousands of other nationalities, with only a small sprinkling of those of American birth. And yet, although the number of Americans is small, the American influence is paramount, and everywhere I went, among high officials or business men, I found a great interest in things American, and an effort to copy after and learn from the institutions in the United States. Their aim is progress and, although some of the methods are rather crude and sometimes impractical, the effort is apparent and great good is being done.

The Tramways, Light and Power Company of São Paulo has had a great influence in this city and has, I believe, been an educational feature in the business development. It is owned by the same group of capitalists who control the company having similar concessions in Rio, but their influence is more easily traced here. The charter of this company is Canadian, but its methods are strictly what we term American, and a number of our fellow-citizens are at work with it. Brazilian young men consider it a credit to be in the employ of this company. They furnish an excellent system of electric traction with about eighty miles of track. The electricity is developed from a waterfall on the Tieté River, a few miles away. A great deal of freight is hauled on the tram lines, and it is no uncommon sight to see car load after car load of squealing pork hauled through the streets.

English is taught in the public schools, and is a required language before a degree is given, so that it will not be many years before the educated classes will all have a knowledge of that language. "And," said the able director of the schools, "we aim to teach a conversational knowledge of the language and not merely a reading knowledge." "Furthermore," he said, "we are copying after the educational methods of the United States just as fast as it is possible to introduce new methods. It can not all be done at once, for certain prejudices exist in favour of the old systems."

BUZZARDS AT THE MARKET, SÃO PAULO.

"*Estado*, Senhor? *Correio?*" These are the cries that greet one's ears as the hustling little newsboys ply their trade, just as their counterparts do in our own land. This city supports a dozen dailies. The two above mentioned are very enterprising publications, which publish more foreign news than the average American daily, although the most of it is European. Then the lotteries are everywhere in evidence. In some blocks there are three or four agencies, besides the vendors on the streets. The Brazilians are born gamblers, and this is their favourite method of wooing the fickle goddess of fortune. There is a national lottery, and perhaps the next most popular one is that of this state. There is a drawing nearly every day, with an occasional grand prize of fifty thousand dollars. I met one American who had just drawn a prize of sixty thousand dollars in the National lottery, and this had caused quite a flutter in the English speaking colony. The people forget that not one dollar is paid out for perhaps four that are paid in, but they are always hoping that the lightning will strike in their direction. Men, women and school children, people in silk and rags, black, white and brown, all buy the little strips of paper with the magic numbers on them, and they eagerly scan the drawings when posted. Brazil is not alone in this folly, however, for all the republics surrounding her encourage the same form of gambling.

As São Paulo is the capital of a state there are the usual public buildings that one will find for the transaction of the public business. The finest and most imposing building in the city is the Municipal Theatre, which is a very fair rival to the one in Rio de Janeiro. It is not quite finished as yet, but the exterior is very fine and in good taste. There are some beautiful homes on the Avenida Tiradentes and the Avenida Paulista, the latter being a comparatively new street. The new thoroughfares are broad and roomy, while the streets in the old town are, for the most part, very narrow and illy adapted for the traffic of a large city. This is overcome to a certain extent by allowing the cars and street traffic to move only one way on many streets.

THE YPIRANGA.

Just beyond São Paulo, and only a short ride by electric car, is a magnificent building known as the Ypiranga, which deserves more than passing notice, for it is built on the site of the birthplace of Brazilian independence. Dom Pedro, representative of the Portuguese authority in Brazil, was also the son of the King of Portugal. In the struggles between

Brazil and the Cortes of Lisbon, which was striving to increase the taxes of that country, and at the same time remove what little constitutional liberty had been granted, this prince was heart and soul on the side of the people. During the long struggle Dom Pedro had ingratiated himself with the people, until all were united with him. Insult was heaped upon the Brazilian deputies in the Cortes, by refusing to let them speak in behalf of their country's cause. At length a peremptory order was sent to Dom Pedro ordering his immediate return to Portugal. The messenger bearing this decree met the prince as he was returning with a hunting party on the bank of a little stream called the "Ypiranga." Upon reading it he called upon his followers, and declared that he would never leave Brazil. "*Independence ou morte* (independence or death), is my watchword," said he. The party took up this watchword, and it spread like wildfire all over the land. This was on the 7th of September, 1822, and a month later Dom Pedro was proclaimed Emperor of Brazil. One will find many streets in Brazil named 7th de Setembro, in commemoration of this *grito*, or shout of independence.

The museum is very imposing, as it stands on an eminence that overlooks the country for miles around. It is built of marble, but the red sand of the country has given it a very peculiar effect, almost like that of old ivory. It contains much that is of scientific interest. Especially fine is the collection of humming birds, beetles and butterflies. There are several specimens of the *Louvadeus* grasshopper, which raises its feelers and poses itself almost in the attitude of prayer. The name means "praise God." One of the principal objects of interest is a large painting representing the scene when the prince pronounced the watchword "independence or death."

GENERAL VIEW OF THE IMMIGRANT STATION AT SÃO PAULO.

The governments of several different states are endeavouring to induce immigrants to come in. The efforts of São Paulo have been most successful, and their methods are copied by other states. This state maintains a splendid immigration office in the city of São Paulo, which is strictly up to date. The immigrants upon landing at Santos are taken by special train to this station, and here they are kept for a week or ten days at government expense. During this time they are housed in excellent quarters, given good food, and kept under the supervision of doctors. Many have had their entire expenses from their homes paid by the government. In these buildings are offices where immigrants are secured employment on the various *fazendas*. A record is kept of each *fazendero* to see if he carries out his contracts. Notices are posted up where labour is wanted on *fazendas* or railroads. Written contracts are made and signed between employer and employee in legal form. The wages generally received are from $.90 to $1.25 per day for such labourers. Interpreters are kept who are able to converse in the many languages that will be required. The labourer is then forwarded to his destination in the interior at government expense. It is far different from the way they are received in our own land, and I only wish that a few hundred thousand of those seeking the shores of the United States each year would turn their steps down this way. They would be better off there than they are in our own great cities.

When I visited this immigration station there were about nine hundred immigrants there who had just been landed. Of this number four-fifths were Spaniards, with a sprinkling of Russians, Poles, Austrians, Hungarians and Italians. A few days later I saw a couple of hundred more of the same varied nationalities landed at Santos, and loaded on a special train for São Paulo. I always pity these poor immigrants who come to a new country with no money, few clothes, many children, and nothing else but a big hope of something, or faith in somebody, in their breast. The total number of immigrants reaching all Brazil in the past year, the excess over those leaving, would not exceed eighty thousand.

The government of São Paulo has established a number of colonies in the state, one or two of which I visited. In these colonies the land is platted in tracts of about fifty acres, which are sold to the colonists at $500 per tract, payable one-tenth each year. The colonist is allowed to live one year free of charge in the colony house, but within this time he must construct his own home. Some of these colonies have proven quite successful, and many immigrants have thus been able to acquire a home with their own vine and fig tree surrounding it. It is certainly the best thing for the colonist, for he has a chance to secure his own home and that ought to be a stimulus to bring out the best there is in a man. In the less developed part of the state, lands will be given the colonist practically free.

The Italian element in Brazil is large, and is increasing each year by immigration. In all of the cities of southern Brazil the Italians are numerous, but they probably reach their largest percentage in the state of São Paulo, where they number about forty per cent. of the population. Of the two and a half millions of people in that state there are perhaps one million of Italian birth. Everywhere one can see evidences of these children of sunny Italy, who have sought homes in the new land because of the overcrowding at home. Most of them come from northern Italy, and they are said to make better workmen than those from Southern Italy. It would be difficult for the coffee planters to work their plantations were it not for these people, and every plantation has one or several colonies of these labourers. They are generally preferred to the negro labourers by the planters. The most of them are industrious and frugal. Many of them eventually join one of the government colonies, and purchase a small tract of land; others become tradesmen, and open a small store to cater to those of their own nationality; still others travel from door to door selling small household articles needed by the housewives. One will hear the same street cries, see the same characteristic packs and bundles, and observe the same styles of dress that are common in the northern provinces of Italy. In recent years the number of Italians coming to Brazil has because of restrictions of the Italian government.

There is still an abundance of soil in this state, nearly three times as large as all New England, awaiting development. The entire western half, which is composed of fertile virgin soil, is practically unexploited. The recent completion of the railroad, which follows the Tieté River to its junction with the Paraná, will open that section to emigration. Along this river, and the other water courses of the state, much fine hardwood timber is found that is well adapted for finishing lumber. Some of the woods are similar to and will take as fine a polish as mahogany. The difficulty is in marketing them. The logs will not float, so that it is necessary to build rafts on which to transport them. As none of the streams flow direct to the Atlantic, the logs must be sent down through the La Plata system, and the many waterfalls make this impracticable. Cheap railroad rates furnish the only solution to this problem.

The water power awaiting development in this state is almost incredible. As the rainfall is large and frequent the volume of water is constant and reliable. On the Tieté River alone there are hundreds of feet of hydraulic falls that could furnish thousands of horsepower energy for practical purposes. The same might be said of the Piracicaba, the Rio Grande, the Paranapanema, and the Mogy-Guassu Rivers, as well as the mighty Paraná itself, which forms the western boundary of São Paulo.

One of the most interesting trips made by me in Brazil was to Riberão Preto, which is in the very centre of the richest coffee district in the world. The route first led over the tracks of the São Paulo Railway to the town of Jundiahy. This line runs through the hills and gradually reaches a lower level. No villages of importance are passed until Jundiahy is reached, and that is interesting only as a railroad junction point. Here a change was made to the Paulista Railway, over which a ride of an hour takes the traveller to

Campinas, a city once very flourishing because the centre of the coffee trade. During the past few years this town has declined, because the coffee production in this neighbourhood has greatly decreased. The city probably contains twenty-five thousand people, and is a typical Brazilian town—far more representative than its more successful rival of São Paulo. There are hundreds of acres of coffee trees still producing in the Campinas district, but they are not well kept, as it seems to be the general intention of abandoning it when the present trees cease to bear. I visited one plantation in this neighbourhood, the Fazenda da Lapa, and it was very interesting, because it was the first one that I had examined, but it cannot compare with the ones later to be described. The charming hospitality of these *fazenderos* is most captivating. On the visit to this plantation the owner served us a meal of fruit fit for a king's table. It was in the early days of January, and we had oranges, bananas, figs, mangoes, pineapples, strawberries, plums and several varieties of grapes, all of them raised on the plantation, and most of which we had ourselves assisted in picking.

THE PICTURESQUE FAZENDA DA LAPA AT CAMPINAS.

At Campinas is located the Instituto Agronomico, which is an experimental institution of the state government. Its purpose is to study the various enemies which attack vegetation and discover means, if possible, for their eradication. It also experiments with the raising of various kinds of grain, and the cultivation of fruits. The work laid out for this institution is a good one, for what is needed in Brazil is a practical application of good agricultural principles, a study of the soil and a knowledge of what it is adapted for. The equipment of this institution is good, and the buildings are large and commodious. But a great deal of money is spent for what might be termed the show features, where it could better be expended for practical purposes. There is a great field, I believe, for the cultivation of fruits. In a country such as this, where fruit trees grow almost without cultivation, a very large percentage of the fruits are imported. For instance, at the hotels the fruit served would be American or Portuguese apples, and Malaga grapes. And yet, right here at this institute, I saw grapes finer, in my opinion, than those brought over thousands of miles of water. With proper cultivation nearly every one of the common fruits of the tropical and temperate zone could be raised here, and of fine quality. Instead, thousands of dollars are sent out of the country for the fruits which might be better raised at home.

From Campinas the journey was continued over the Mogyana Railroad, a narrow gauge track. The line passes through coffee plantations for some distance, and then into uncultivated lands, where the only industry is the raising of stock. A part of the land traversed is abandoned agricultural land, and part of it has never been under cultivation. The cattle seen on these farms are only of fair quality, for not much care has been taken in breeding the animals up to a high standard. With many bends and graceful curves the road follows a stream, cuts across valleys and around hills. There is no part of the ten hours' journey when hills of fair size are not a prominent feature in the foreground. A number of towns are passed, and a few very narrow gauged railroads run off to plantations, which cannot be seen from the railroads. The soil is almost the colour of dried blood, and this red dirt filters in through the windows in great clouds. This blood-red dust colours everything it touches with a reddish hue. The clothing is soon tinted with it, and even the children's complexions show the effects, for Brazilian children, like their cousins all over the world, like to play in the dirt. But this red soil is good coffee land, and coffee plantations are seen crowning the summits of the hills. At last the train reaches Riberão Preto, near which are situated the best and largest coffee plantations, not only in Brazil but in the world. The town is comparatively modern, for this district is newer than Campinas, and it has been growing in importance year after year in the past two decades. It is now a city of ten or fifteen thousand people.

"MONTE ALEGRE" FAZENDA.

At the station were waiting carriages from the hospitable "Monte Alegre" *fazenda,* the residence of Colonel Francisco Schmidt, who is known as the "coffee king." This man came to Brazil as a poor emigrant boy a half century ago, and hoed coffee trees for other *fazenderos,* and on lands which he now owns. Seated on the broad veranda of "Monte Alegre," one could see avenues of coffee trees stretching out over the hills, and good coffee lands are always hilly, until they were lost in the horizon. Although it was not possible to see, yet one knew that they continued in the same unbroken rows down the other slope. I rode in a carriage with the Colonel for hours through a continuous succession of coffee trees, during the three days that I was his guest, with no end in sight. When you consider that there are from two hundred and fifty to three hundred trees to each acre, you will readily realize that the number of trees soon runs into the thousands, then into the tens of thousands, and finally into the millions. So do not be surprised when I tell you that this coffee king has already growing upon his various *fazendas* the almost incredible number of eight million coffee trees. I did not see all of them, but I saw so many that numbers lost their meaning, and I could only think in millions.

Twenty-three million pounds of coffee were marketed by this man in one year. This is enough to give every man, woman and child in the United States and Canada a cup of coffee for breakfast for one week. He has twenty railroad stations on his thirty-two different *fazendas*. He has twenty machines run by water or steam power for cleaning coffee, and acres upon acres of drying yards, all of which are scenes of activity in the harvesting season. Nearly a thousand horses are employed in the work of the plantations, besides more than that number of mules and oxen. There is also a fully-equipped sugar mill, which turns out thousands of pounds of refined sugar each year. In fact, the Colonel told me, as we were seated at the great dining table, that would seat forty persons, and which was spread with the good things of life: "Everything on the table, except the flour used in making the bread, was raised on this plantation."

The Colonel reminded me of the feudal lords of old, for the eight thousand people who live on his plantations not only depend on him for labour, but look up to him and tip their hats respectfully whenever they see him. The work of taking care of the coffee trees is all let out to families at so much a thousand trees per year, and a family will take care of five thousand trees. The price paid is from $25.00 to $30.00 per thousand per year for hoeing and cleaning the fields, and they are paid in addition to this for picking the coffee at established rates. Furthermore, they are permitted to plant corn and beans in between the coffee rows which gives them an extra profit. Day labourers are paid at the rate of $.90 to $1.00 for each day's work.

Everything about this plantation is conducted in a systematic manner, and in that is the secret of Colonel Schmidt's success. The thirty-two farms are all connected with his home by telephone, for which more than eighty miles of telephone wire have been strung. Everything, including plumbing supplies, is kept in systematic order and the owner himself knows where each article may be found. Machinery when not in use is carefully stored under shelter to protect it from rust. A half dozen blacksmiths, as many woodworkers, harnessworkers, shoemakers, etc., are kept on the plantation, and even a private tailor is employed at the house. A dozen or more general stores are operated for supplying the wants of the employees. With this and much more detail this great plantation is run on modern business methods, with as perfect a system of bookkeeping as the average business man employs. From these books can be told at a glance the exact cost of each plantation for each year, its production and the net profit to the owner. And, above all, the Colonel is a charming host, and finds time to make it interesting for those, like myself, who visit him where he is king.

A RUBBER PLANTATION OF MANIÇOBA RUBBER TREES.

The "Dumont" *fazenda* adjoins the one just described, and it is the second largest plantation in Brazil, and perhaps in the world. It was formerly owned by the family of Santos-Dumont, the aeronaut, but is now under the control of an English company. They own a private railroad with more than forty miles of track, which runs to Riberão Preto. The track is only twenty-six inches wide, and the cars are rather narrow with room for only one person on each side of the aisle. A special train, with the best car the road possesses, drawn by a Baldwin engine, was sent for us and we were taken over the coffee plantation, which possesses nearly five million trees. It was also very interesting to travel over the thousands of acres owned by them, in and through the rows of coffee trees which almost brushed up against the car in places, in this comfortable, if diminutive coach, and see the methods of culture and care of the coffee, which is slightly different than that pursued on the other. It was also interesting to find an up-to-date American in charge of the vast interests of this English company, and to know that one of our own nationality is making good in the coffee-raising industry as well as in other lines. This company markets all its own coffee through an auxiliary company in England in packages under its own labels. The "Dumont" *fazenda* is also conducting an experiment in rubber culture, and now has forty thousand trees growing, some of which are almost ready to tap. If rubber continues to advance, as it has in the past year, this part of their plantation may prove more profitable than the growing of coffee.

CHAPTER VII
AN AMERICAN COLONY UNDER THE SOUTHERN CROSS

Have you ever heard of the Villa Americana in Brazil?

Quite likely you have not, for I had never heard of it myself until my visit to that interesting country brought it to my notice. We frequently hear of German villages, Hungarian settlements and Italian colonies, but a settlement of North Americans on the other side of the equator is something new. And yet the colony is not new, for it was established more than a generation ago; children have grown up and married, who still call themselves North Americans, and who have never set foot on soil over which waves the stars and stripes. In travelling over Brazil I frequently met with American young men and women who informed me that they came from the Villa Americana. So often did that name reach my ears that I decided to visit this place, and see for myself what kind of a settlement it was, and how these voluntarily expatriated fellow countrymen lived in this land so different from our own. It is a journey of about two hours from Campinas on the Paulista Railway.

But first let me tell you the history of this colony. At the close of the civil war many Southern families, whose plantations had been devastated by the northern armies, felt that they could not live again under the old flag. Proud spirited and unconquered, these brave southern veterans who had marched with Stonewall Jackson, and the Lees, and Johnsons, decided that they would leave the land that had given them birth and seek fortunes anew in a new land, and amidst new surroundings. Brazil appealed to the leaders in this movement because the plantation system was similar to that under which they had been raised, and slavery was legal in that land, which was still an empire. A few men went as an advance guard and selected a site about one hundred miles northwest of the city of São Paulo. A favourable report was made to those still back in the States, and it was not long until several hundred families had left their Southern homes, and were making new homes underneath the Southern Cross. In all it is estimated that at least five hundred American families located in that section of the state of São Paulo, Brazil, between the years 1865 and 1870. They came from Texas, Georgia, Alabama, Tennessee, and perhaps one or two other of the seceding states.

As I stepped off the *rapido,* as the express train is called down there, the name Villa Americana, which means American Village, on the neat little station struck a sympathetic chord in my heart. It seemed good also to see a number of tall, slender men, typical Southern types, such as one might see at almost any station in Tennessee or Georgia, standing on the platform awaiting the incoming train. One member of the colony, who was in the government employ, was with me and performed the introductions necessary. "How do you do," "Glad to see you," "Come around and see me," and similar cordial expressions came from every one. And the best of it is that they were sincere, and not the empty, meaningless expressions so often heard. It was a pleasure to accept several of these invitations, as many as my limited time allowed.

VIEW IN VILLA AMERICANA.

On entering the home of perhaps the most prosperous member of this colony I felt like standing at "attention," and giving a salute when I saw the silk starred and striped banner of Uncle Sam fastened up on the wall of the "best room." The house itself, with its large hall, roomy apartments and broad veranda surrounding the house, looked like one of the plantation houses so common in the South. This man had a large family of children, all of whom, with one exception, had been educated in the schools of the United States, and two boys were at that time in one of our colleges. About the whole house was an American atmosphere that warmed the very heart's blood in a traveller so far away from home. And so it was in the other houses I visited; in every one was the same cordiality, the same pleasure at seeing some one from the "States," and the same loyalty to everything American. In some of the younger members one could detect a slight accent in speaking English, which is always noticeable when children learn a Latin tongue in their babyhood. The older ones said that these young people speak the Portuguese with a similar foreign accent. The young ladies of the American colony, and there are a number of them, were typical American girls, bright, cheery and free as their sisters are at home, and so different from the Brazilian young women among whom they live, and who are so hampered by the customs and traditions of the race. We took a "trolley" ride over the settlement, but it is rather different from the American trolley, for it is nothing more than an old-fashioned buckboard.

Many of the original members of the colony became dissatisfied, and returned to their former homes. There are, however, four or five hundred Americans still living in this colony, or within a radius of a few miles. A few have moved to other parts of Brazil, and others have intermarried with Brazilians; but, in general, they have remained true to their Americanism. Some of the original families purchased slaves and worked their plantations in that way, until that institution was abolished in 1888. A few have prospered very much, but many others have done just fairly well. One of the wealthiest men made his little fortune out of watermelons. Others have sugar plantations and make brandy, or raise coffee; and still others do general farming, similar to what they were accustomed in the Southern States. A Protestant church, called the Union Church, adorns one hill, and a school-house in a conspicuous building is in another part of the village.

A BRAZILIAN FRUIT MARKET. MELONS FROM VILLA AMERICANA.

Some one had told me that the war was a tabooed subject; that the few older members still left were fighting the battles over. When I met the oldest member of the colony, who had left the United States in 1865, the impulse came to test this subject. I mentioned the fact that my own father had served in the Union army and fought for his country on that side. This old man, who was past the allotted three score and ten, and who had fought with that intrepid warrior, Stonewall Jackson, then told me the whole history of the colony, and the causes that led to its establishment. "It was a mistake," he said, "but we did not realize it then, and afterwards it was too late to sacrifice what we had here and move back. We still love the old flag." When I left, he gave me the Brazilian embrace as a special mark of favour; and I verily believe that I left a good friend in this old man who had the traits that we all love in the Southern gentleman.

When Senator Root, then Secretary of State, visited Brazil four years ago, a new station was named Elihu Root in his honour on the Paulista Railway, and this name stands out conspicuously on every time-table of that line. The special train conveying him passed through the Villa Americana, and he was asked to stop and address the Americans. When the train stopped many of the older residents met him with tears in their eyes; and, I was told, the eyes of the distinguished American were not dry; and he has said that it was the most pathetic incident in his trip. He was asked whether it would be better for the colony to remain in Brazil or return to the United States. "Stay where you are," he said, "and be good Brazilians. You will find the States so changed that they would no longer seem like home."

The Secretary was right. A few months before my own visit one of the prosperous members of the colony went, with his family, to his old home in Texas, with the intention of remaining there. He left his property in the hands of an agent for sale. A few weeks after his arrival in Texas he cabled to his agent not to sell the property, as he was coming back. In a few months he and his family returned to the Villa, giving as his reason that the old neighbourhood had changed so much that it did not seem so much like home as Brazil.

The members of this colony are now Brazilian subjects, the younger ones because of their birth in that land, and the older ones by virtue of a general proclamation. Few of them actually take any part in the politics of the land. All of them, of course, speak the Portuguese language, but use the English in their homes. They are still Americans at heart. My visit to this little American settlement in the very heart of the great Republic of Brazil will always remain a pleasant memory of a most delightful trip.

CHAPTER VIII
THE TEMPERATE ZONE

Brazil is not all within the tropics. The Tropic of Capricorn passes through the suburbs of the city of São Paulo. South of this line is the temperate zone, within which is included the states of Santa Catharina and Rio Grande do Sul, almost the entire state of Paraná, and a part of the states of São Paulo and Matto Grosso. Leaving São Paulo, a ride of two hours over a unique railroad carries the traveller to the busiest port in Brazil. The ride down the Serro is delightful on a clear day. The train is divided into small sections, each with its own powerful little engine, which are attached to a cable. One section is always taken up while another is going down in order to balance the load. Through tunnels, over tressels and along shelves cut out of the solid rock, the train gradually descends until the coast level is reached, and a short ride carries the traveller into the splendid station at Santos.

The city of Santos is not alone one of the most important ports of Brazil, but of the world as well, because of the enormous quantity of coffee shipped from it. At one time it was noted in a different way. It was then regarded as one of the most unhealthy cities in the Americas. I talked with a man who had lived there for twenty-five years, and he told me that in times of pestilence the dead bodies would be taken out to the cemetery by the score each day. People who went there hardly dared to breathe, so fearful were they of contagion. The Brazilian government deserves great credit for the changes that have been wrought in Santos, for the death rate is no greater than in the average coast city, as complete sanitation has been effected, and a good water supply brought in.

The name of Santos is an abbreviation of the original name Todos os Santos (All the Saints), for it was on All Saints' Day that the site was discovered by Braz Cubras, in 1543. It was plundered by the English Vice-Admiral Cook in 1651, under orders from Admiral Thomas Cavendish. Because of its admirable bay Santos early became an important port. It is situated on a point of land which becomes an island in the rainy season. It looks quite picturesque as one sails up the channel to the docks, with the tropical vegetation and the surrounding hills which slope almost to the water's edge.

It is the only harbour along the Atlantic coast where vessels can unload without resort to lighters. A very extensive system of docks has been constructed here, which will be two and one-half miles in length when finished. Several dozen vessels will then be able to lay at the wharf at the same time, as frequently happens in the busy season. More than one thousand boats call here each year. The city is not especially interesting, as there is nothing to distinguish it from other Brazilian cities. The main interest lies along the docks. And, by the way, the Docas de Santos Company have a contract that is worth a fortune. This company constructed the docks, and are given a concession which is bringing in millions of dollars in profit.

LOADING COFFEE AT SANTOS DOCKS.

In the coffee season the docks, the streets of the shipping quarter and the warehouses have a busy appearance. The streets are almost rendered impassable by the wagons loaded with bags of coffee. Dozens of *carigadores* hurry back and forth between the wagons and warehouses, or between warehouses and boats, with two or three bags of coffee on their shoulders. Women dart here and there among the wagons, and pick, or scrape up, the berries which have been spilled upon the ground during the loading and unloading; and they sometimes realize a fair sum for a day's work. In the warehouses the coffee is emptied out in immense piles, sorted and resacked in bags of uniform weight, and then stacked up in piles which number thousands of bags. From these docks the coffee is sent out to Europe and America, and from there distributed to all parts of the civilized world.

The through steamers to Argentina and Uruguay do not stop at any Brazilian ports south of Santos, so that it is necessary to take the national boats. It is a law of the country that coast steamers must fly the Brazilian flag. There are two lines that make the various stops, of which the Costeira Line of Lage Brothers is probably the best, as they have English captains.

After leaving Santos the tropical plants and palms grow less luxuriantly, and the vegetation more closely resembles our Gulf States. The first port at which the boat stops is Paranaguá, the only harbour, and the only port of any importance on the coast of the state of Paraná, a state about the size of Pennsylvania. There is a strip of lowland along the coast that is subtropical, being low, flat and marshy. On these marsh lands rice has been very successfully cultivated during the past few years. West of the coast range of mountains the climate is more temperate, and there are some fine plateaus that extend as far as the Paraná River on the western boundary.

CUTTING RICE WITH AN AMERICAN HARVESTER.

Paranaguá is a thriving town of ten thousand or more, and has one of the finest harbours on the coast. From this port a railway has been built to the capital, Curytiba, and Ponta Grossa, the second largest town in the state, a distance of nearly two hundred miles. This line is a triumph of engineering, for it climbs over the Serro da Mar without resorting to the aid of cogs or cables. A ride over it affords some magnificent views in the richness and variety of views to be seen as the train runs around bends, and bursts forth from the many tunnels along the line. This route is said to have been the scene of many tragic deaths during the revolution of 1893-4, when revolutionists were carried by train to the highest points along the line, and then brutally hurled into the depths below.

It is a journey of about four hours to Curytiba, which is a pretty little city of half a hundred thousand people, more or less. It is one of the largest cities south of São Paulo, and is situated at an altitude of 2,500 feet above sea level, thus giving it a pleasant and equable temperature. The city is comparatively modern with the usual public buildings of a capital, plazas filled with shrubbery and flowers, and a Botanical Garden of which the people are very proud.

Paraná is a rich state in natural resources. It was formerly united with São Paulo as one province, and the original inhabitants have many of the same qualities as the Paulistas. Many foreign colonies have been established by state aid, and some of them have prospered. Italians, Poles and Germans constitute the colonists, of whom the Poles are probably the most numerous. There are large areas of forests, of which a tree known as the Paraná pine is the most common, as well as most useful. This tree grows to a lofty and imposing height, with a trunk several feet thick. It is used much the same as our own pine, and a great deal of it is exported to the other Brazilian states, as well as to Argentina and Uruguay.

The most valuable article of commerce at the present time is the *Ilex Paraguayensis*, from which the herb maté, or Paraguay tea, is made. Brazil is a great producer of this tea as well as coffee. From this maté is brewed a beverage that is used by twenty million or more of South Americans, for one will see its disciples in Brazil, Paraguay, Uruguay, Chile and Argentina, and probably other countries as well. The early Jesuit missionaries were the first discoverers of the virtue of this plant, when they found the Indians chewed it, and by doing so were able to undergo great hardships with very little solid food. These fathers experimented with the shrub, or rather tree, and instructed the Indians in its cultivation. At a later time immense forests were discovered, and it is from them that the principal crop is now obtained.

The state of Paraná produces more of this preparation than any other country, and several million dollars' worth of it are shipped each year to the other states and foreign countries. Its production has been the source of wealth to not a few in that state, for the *yerbales*, as the plantations are called, have proven very profitable. It is made from the leaves of a tree that is generally about the size of an orange tree, but will sometimes grow to a height of twenty-five feet, and with a trunk two, and even three feet, in circumference. One tree will oftentimes yield ninety pounds of the prepared herb. As the plantations are generally remote, the gatherers go together in their long trips across country. The season begins in December, and lasts for a number of months. Firing, and in some places, the picking, drying and packing were all formerly done on the grounds, but now machinery has been installed for the different processes of preparing it for the market. By the old process the maté gatherers cleared off a space of ground, and then beat it down very hard. The freshly cut stems and leaves were first placed in the centre and a fire built around it; then placed on poles with a fire underneath. Drying the leaves two or three days reduced them to a dry powder, and they were then packed in bags made ready to be taken back to the markets. Large copper pans placed over a slow fire now take the place of this primitive process.

A number of scientists claim high medicinal qualities for the beverage. They say that it has more stimulating and tonic effects than the common tea, with absolutely none of the bad or unpleasant effects. Instead of keeping the user awake, for instance, it is claimed that the user is never troubled with insomnia. It can be made and used the same as any tea, but it is commonly taken from the *cuya*, and drawn up through the *bombilla*. The *cuya* is a small bowl or gourd, with a little opening through which the maté is put in. Hot water is then poured over, and a little sugar added. The *bombilla* is a small pipe, with a strainer on the end, through which the beverage is sipped. Some of these *cuyas* and *bombillas* are very elaborate and made of pure silver. Hot water and another lump of sugar must be added every few minutes to keep it palatable. It is a very common sight to see the natives sitting outside their homes sipping this favourite drink of theirs, its use oftentimes supplanting the stronger intoxicants. Some hotels and restaurants serve it, and many foreigners become as fond of maté as those who were born in the country, and its use is being introduced in a small way in Europe.

As the vessel proceeds farther south it stops at Florianapolis, capital of the state of Santa Catharina. The coast of this state is, perhaps, the most beautiful of all the Brazilian states, excepting that of Rio de Janeiro. The maritime range rises very abruptly to a great height, with only a very narrow strip between it and the sea. There are several good harbours. Florianapolis lies on an island, about five miles from the mainland which the city faces. It makes a beautiful picture. Where Rio is grand, there is a softness about this scene that also appeals to the poetic side of nature. Back of the city rises the background of hills, green with semi-tropical verdure, which reach a height of three thousand feet. The entire island is almost a garden of beauty with its variegated hues of shrubs and flowers, and the driveways which are overhung with trees and vines. It is not as large as Curytiba, but is more important in a commercial sense than that neighbouring capital, because it is a shipping port at which several vessels call each week.

The state of Santa Catharina is somewhat similar to Paraná, although not so large. The plateaus are devoted to stock raising, of which horses and mules form a large part. The majority of the small but tough and wiry mules used in the states farther north come from this state. Some tobacco, sugar and dairy products are also exported, and fruit is now being cultivated on a much larger scale than formerly. A number of German colonies are found in this state, and some of them are so pronouncedly Teutonic that the Portuguese tongue is scarcely understood. This shows not only in the architecture of these towns, but also in the dress and manners of the inhabitants, although the greater part of the German element has lived here for a long time. Joinville, Blumenau and Brusque are three of these distinctly German settlements. It is a question whether they have advanced faster than the native Brazilians. At least it is certain that they have not kept pace with the Fatherland, probably because there has been no continued influx of new blood into the settlements.

Leaving Florianapolis the vessel skirts along the shores of Santa Catharina, and for a long distance along the low coast of the state of Rio Grande do Sul, until the port of the same name, the most southerly port of the republic, is reached. The coast line of this state is peculiar in that it consists of lakes or lagoons, which are separated from the sea by comparatively narrow strips of land. The principal lake, called Lagoa dos Patos (Ducks Lake), is one hundred and fifty miles long and from twenty to thirty miles wide, and has only one narrow channel connecting it with the ocean, that at Rio Grande do Sul, at its southerly extremity. The lake is not very deep, but a twelve foot channel has been dredged to Pelotas, and a ten foot channel has been completed almost to Porto Alegre. At the entrance there are sandbars which make it impossible for deep draught vessels to enter, but the coasting boats proceed up to the furthermost extremity, at which is located the largest city of the state, Porto Alegre, the "merry port."

The government is now engaged in the work of dredging a channel to a depth of ten meters (thirty-two and eight-tenths feet) over this bar which, with the port works planned, will give Rio Grande do Sul one of the best harbours on the Brazilian coast, and will probably make it the chief city south of São Paulo. The cost of this improvement will be about $10,000,000 in gold, for which a special tax of two per cent. on all goods coming into the state through this channel has been levied. The port works will cost almost an equal sum, and a concession has been granted to a company which agrees to make this improvement. The plan adopted is to construct two parallel dikes, or jetties, from the mouth of the river into the new harbour, and there construct basins which will be large enough to manœuvre the largest vessels afloat. Rubble stones and immense cement blocks will be used for this work, and it is estimated that at least four million tons of this material will be required. At least ten million cubic yards will have to be dredged for the channel and basins. The sand and clay brought up by the dredges will be deposited inside the revetments in order to fill up the low land. This improvement was formally begun December 11th, 1907, and the preliminary work has been done, so that the main part of the undertaking is now progressing very satisfactorily. An American engineer is in charge of the work, but the contract is held by a French company. It is expected that this much needed improvement, which has been under consideration for a quarter of a century, will be completed in 1913. This will revolutionize this port and make Rio Grande do Sul a port of call for European and American steamers. It will not only give an easy outlet to Southern Brazil, but a much shorter one for Northern Uruguay and a part of Argentina.

Rio Grande do Sul of to-day is a thrifty little city of twenty-five thousand inhabitants, with pretty parks and narrow streets, but nothing outside of its shipping to attract much attention to itself. There are schools, colleges and churches, charitable institutions and a library, all of which are excellent in themselves. It is about eight hundred miles from Rio harbour. A decade hence it will be a much more important and a much larger city than at present. A few miles farther up the lake is the larger town of Pelotas, which is the centre of the beef curing establishments, of which there are so many along this lake. In addition to the beef consumed locally these *xarqueados* prepare and export more than $6,000,000 worth of this dried and salted meat annually.

The southern part of Rio Grande do Sul is composed of prairie lands, called *campos*, which comprise perhaps two-thirds of the area of this state, which is twice as large as the state of New York. These plains are covered with pasture, and contain only a little timber along the streams. These great *campos* are divided up into *estancias* or *fazendas*, which are frequently many thousands of acres in extent. Natural boundaries, such as streams and ridges, have generally been chosen, which not only serve as natural fences, but settle absolutely all questions of ownership. The house of the *estanciero* is generally situated on an elevation which overlooks the estate, and around it are grouped the huts of the labourers. There is, as a rule, no cultivation of the soil except to supply the wants of those dwelling on the estate. The entire attention is devoted to the raising of cattle, of which there are more than four million in the state. A few raise mules to supply the cities. The *Rio Grandense*, as the inhabitant is called, is, first of all, a ranchman.

In the spring, men, called the *tropeiros*, visit all the *estancias*, and bargain for the cattle at so much a head for cash. They are then formed into great herds and driven overland to the *xarqueados*, which is the name given to the killing establishments of Brazil. In these establishments the salted and dried beef is prepared, which forms the principal meat supply of central and northern Brazil, where few cattle are raised.

SELLING CATTLE IN RIO GRANDE DO SUL.

The process of preparing this meat is quite interesting, for it is so much different from the methods of preparing and preserving beef in our own country. Pelotas is the greatest centre of this industry, but thousands of head of cattle are also killed at Bagé, Quarahim, San Gabriel and other towns. The work of killing and curing is done in the season from November to May, which are the summer months. After an animal has been killed the carcass is taken to a long and broad dissecting shed, where it is immediately set upon by a man and boys armed with long knives. In less than ten minutes, as a rule, the hide has been removed, and all the meat cut in strips and removed from the bones. These strips of meat are made as large as possible. After being cut up the strips are hung up for a time on poles to cool, but no artificial cooling process is used. They are then immersed in immense tanks filled with strong salt brine. Later, they are placed in a tank filled with a still stronger brine, and, finally, into a third solution of great strength.

After being sufficiently soaked in this strong brine, the strips of meat are piled up with alternate layers of salt. From these piles the meat is laid out on rows of railings, and thoroughly dried in the sun, which gives it the final process of curing and seasoning. This meat then becomes the *xarque*, or jerked beef, which forms a most important article of food in Brazil, and can be seen for sale in the meat markets all over the country. It is bound in bales of about two hundred pounds, covered with sacking and shipped to the markets. To use it the meat must first be soaked for a time in water to remove the excess of the salt preservative, and then it is boiled or roasted, making a nutritive diet of which the people are very fond. The tongues are prepared in the same way, and shipped to the northern markets. The hides are salted to preserve them, the bones, horns and hoofs are boiled to remove all the tallow and glue, and all of these products are shipped to Europe. The process as followed to this day is a wasteful one. The same care and economy of manufacture followed in the United States would yield far greater profits to the manufacturers. A half million or more of cattle are slaughtered and cured in this way, in the state of Rio Grande do Sul each year, and it could be developed to far greater proportions under proper management. It will not be, however, until foreign capital develops the industry, as it has in Argentina.

VIEW OF PORTO ALEGRE.

At the northern end of the lagoon is the principal city of Southern Brazil, Porto Alegre. It is a neat and prosperous city, in which nearly all the foreign banks and business houses doing business in Brazil have branches. The view in travelling up the lagoon is not especially attractive, for it consists mostly of flat fields along which are miles of racks, on which the jerked beef is laid out to dry. The city itself is built on a promontory which juts out into the river. The commercial prosperity of this city began with the colonizing of a lot of Germans soon after the revolution of the middle of the last century in Germany. The Teutonic element is very marked in Porto Alegre, as well as in other cities of the state, such as Novo Friburgo and São Leopoldo, which are still more distinctly German. There is a large municipal theatre, city hall, cathedral and other public buildings. In fact, commercially as well as in every other way, Porto Alegre is the leading city south of São Paulo.

Rio Grande do Sul has a population of about a million and a quarter, thus making it fifth in population in the republic. Its climate is temperate, and the winter season sometimes becomes quite cool. Snow occasionally falls, and, when the cold winds blow in from the west, the still waters freeze over. It resembles very much the plains of Uruguay, on which also immense herds of cattle feed. A number of minerals are found, and it contains about the only profitable coal mines that have yet been discovered in Brazil. Near Porto Alegre are some coal mines that have been worked for years; but they are not worked near to their full capacity, because the freight rates are so high that the coal cannot be shipped profitably to the other Brazilian states. A little gold is mined as well as some silver, lead and copper. A number of precious stones such as amethysts, topaz, tourmalines, aquamarines and moonstones are found in certain sections.

Rio Grande do Sul has had a chequered career almost ever since its settlement. For a long time its ownership was contested between Spaniards and Portuguese, although at an earlier time, when the capitancias were formed, no one considered it worth the taking. Many of the original settlers came from the Azores, and some of the inhabitants are still glad to call themselves Azoreans. It was not until 1822 that it was definitely united with the rest of Brazil, but at that time it was joined to the empire as a separate province. The independent and martial spirit, engendered by the many wars, has made the state very independent, and this has caused it to be turbulent.

Quite a good deal of railway construction has been done in the past decade, and this has added to the prosperity of the country by opening up new districts to trade and commerce. The construction of railways is comparatively easy. The Uruguay River on the western boundary furnishes good communication with Uruguayan and Argentinian ports, and regular steamship service is maintained on it. There are also some rivers emptying into the lake, which are navigable for small craft.

The state of Matto Grosso, (the dense forest) is an empire in itself, for it contains a greater area than the original thirteen colonies. It is one-sixth as large as the United States. It is not only an undeveloped, but practically an unexplored country, whose resources are only half understood. Much of it is as wild as it was when Sebastian Cabot made his way up the Paraguay River early in the sixteenth century. All of its supplies are conveyed up the waterways of the La Plata system, and it takes a month to reach Cuyaba, the capital, from Rio de Janeiro. It has a population not exceeding one person to each four square miles of territory, so that there are few towns. Cuyaba has perhaps twenty thousand souls, and has long ago passed the century mark of its existence. It is said to be quite an attractive little city.

It is a five days' ride from Rio to Buenos Ayres. From there it is a journey of about six days up the Paraná and Paraguay Rivers to Ascuncion, the capital of the Republic of Paraguay. A two days' ride above Ascuncion carries one within the borders of Matto Grosso. The Paraguay River, which, up to this point, has been wide, gradually narrows. The scenery becomes wilder, and the river runs between mountains, at the base of which grow giant palms and tree-like ferns. Vines and creepers bind together the tall trees, which stand in a mass of impenetrable vegetation. The only break in this is an occasional farmhouse along the bank. Many kinds of wild birds and some wild animals are seen, alligators abound in the water and fish are plentiful. The jaguar is not uncommon. It is only after several changes of steamers, and a journey of twenty-seven hundred miles by river boats, that one at last reaches the capital of this monstrous province. The Paraguay River is well adapted to navigation. As far as Ascuncion it has a depth of at least twenty feet. For several hundred miles above this city the depth never goes below twelve feet. There are few islands and it is more easy of navigation than the Paraná, which is so much obstructed by shoals and rapids. This fortunate natural outlet will render a cheap and easy transportation for the produce of this state when developed. The northern part of this state drains into the Amazon, and a number of the rivers are navigable almost to the centre of the state.

CHAPTER IX
THE AMAZON

What a prospect of unlimited forest greets the visitor to the Amazon. What a land of dreams and mysteries is unfolded. Three or four hundred miles to the south, and as great a distance to the north, stretches an unbroken forest and jungle, until one reaches the open plateaus of Matto Grosso, on one side, or the boundaries of Venezuela and the Guianas, on the other. To the west there are trees and trees, set close together, and mingling their boughs with the intertwining vines into a vegetable infinity. Much of it is still an unknown land, untrodden by the foot of white man. The tangle has been threaded at different places by exploring expeditions and the rubber gatherers, but to the world it is still an unconversant wilderness. A traveller finds vegetation of one kind on one river, and the same form on another stream a hundred miles away. He then infers that all the intervening territory has the same character, and so reports it. He may be right; and again he may be mistaken.

In the regions between ten degrees on either side of the equator lies the major part of this primeval forest. Forest and rivers alike depend on the rain. The moist trade winds, which blow westward from the Atlantic, meet the cold blasts from the lofty, snow-capped Andes, and precipitation follows. The forests protect the rivers by preventing evaporation, and the rivers nurse the trees by increasing the moisture in soil and air. Thus this region, which has the greatest rainfall in the world, has produced the mightiest river and the largest stretch of forest on the globe.

Like a huge wall rise the tall trees on every hand. A photograph of a thousand feet of the bank at one place would answer for the same amount of bank at any other place, except that the palms might predominate in some places more than at others. There are no solitary tree trunks; neither are there groups of trees of the same species. It would scarcely be possible to find a half-dozen trees of the same kind to the acre. Penetrate this forest and you have the feeling of having entered a maze or a web. There are plants and trunks but no leaves near the ground. It is the vines that cause one to feel that he has been entrapped. Vines are here, there and everywhere. The great tree trunks are wreathed with them, and the branches above are woven together with them into a labyrinth of leaves and stems. They are not little puny stems, such as may be found in our northern woods, but many of them are giants with woody fibre, almost like that of the tree trunks themselves. They ascend one tree and stretch across a half a dozen others; and then may drop down to the ground again. They are twisted, knotted and looped into almost every conceivable shape. Some have smooth stems and others are covered with spines; some are round or square, and others are gathered together into bundles.

Follow up the vines for fifty feet and you meet with the parasites in countless variety. They are grouped, massed and interwoven; they cling to the trees wherever there is a chance, and feed on the moist air. There are hundreds of cord-like air-roots which dangle in the air, and others send a branch down to mother earth for sustenance. Delicate orchids bloom among the other plants on the branches. Many trees depend more on the air than soil for sustenance. Cut a tree, and it will probably remain green and throw off new branches. Then further up one will see the green roof composed of the matted leaves and vines, which almost exclude the light from the ground below. Some of the largest trees spread over the others a wide, thick roof of verdure, like a vast umbrella. The mighty columnar stems, which bear aloft this solid roof of lofty green, would make the proudest of earth's beings feel awed and humbled. The visitor to these forests feels his own insignificance. It is almost impossible to keep in a straight line, for in some places the thickets are too dense to be passable. You feel your loneliness. At sea or on the desert one has a definite horizon, a fixed boundary. Here you are absolutely separated from the world. The thicket is so compact that oftentimes it is impossible to see more than a score of feet. An army of men could not find you, and, unless an experienced woodman, it would be almost impossible to find the way by yourself. One can only tramp along hour after hour, cutting the narrow path as well as possible, but seeing only an interminable stretch of unbroken forest ahead as far as the eye can penetrate.

The jaguar, called by the natives *onca*, as well as several other species of these cat-like animals, are encountered in these forests. The commonest variety is almost as large as the Asiatic tiger and is sometimes almost as dangerous. The tapir is the largest animal found in South America, and it frequents these Amazonian jungles. It is, however, a sluggish animal, something like a large hog, but a dangerous fighter when cornered. Monkeys abound, and their strange human-like faces may be seen gazing down upon the unwelcome intruders from the lofty branches above. The natives are very fond of certain species, which they esteem a great delicacy. Small red deer are also found, but they are not so palatable as our northern species. The paca is a rodent about two feet long, and is considered a choice delicacy. They look very much like a rat except that they are spotted and tailless. The sloth is one of nature's curiosities which seems to have been left over from a prehistoric age. It is not only peculiar in looks, with its little round bullet-like head, but is as peculiar in its habits. It always hangs upside down on a limb, and lives all its days in a sort of dead calm between eating and sleeping. It is likely to fall asleep between steps in moving from one place to another. After taking a few steps the sloth will probably fall in almost a state of exhaustion. Its utmost speed would probably be fifteen or twenty feet in an hour on the ground. Like some kinds of insects, they are distasteful to other animals, and carnivorous beasts will eat them only as a last resort. They are sluggish and very hard to kill, for their circulation seems to be as sluggish as their movements. The ant-bear is another strange animal occasionally encountered, and is very valuable, for it lives entirely on those pestering insects. The peccary, armadillo, capivara and tatou are other animals peculiar to these forests. Lizards are very numerous. In size they vary from the little house lizards, which dart out from dark corners, to the big fat ones two feet long which the natives prize very highly.

In the number and variety of fishes the Amazon is especially prolific. Agassiz says: "The Amazon nourishes about twice as many species as the Mediterranean, and a more considerable number than the Atlantic Ocean from one pole to the other. All the rivers of Europe combined, from the Tagus to the Volga, do not feed more than one hundred and fifty species of fresh water fish, and yet in one little lake in the neighbourhood of Manaos we have discovered more than two hundred species, the greater part of which have not yet been observed elsewhere." The largest is the river cow, or manatee, which is really a mammal, although it never leaves the water. This fish, or animal, oftentimes obtains a length of fifteen feet, and the meat is said to taste very much like coarse pork. The most valuable fish from a food standpoint is the pirarucu, which often grows to seven feet in length, and weighs as much as two hundred and twenty pounds. It has an elongated snout covered with bony plates or scales, the body being cylindrical. It is generally caught with a harpoon in clear water. The salted and dried meat brings a good price, and is sold everywhere along the Amazon, making one of the principal articles of food. The piranha is a salmon-like fish, which is rather feared for it has a habit of biting pieces of flesh from the limbs of bathers. It is very voracious in its eating and will take almost any kind of bait. In some places the natives capture a supply of fish by pouring the juice of a vine into the water, which seems to have the effect of an anæsthetic upon them. Turtles also abound, and are considered a great delicacy by the natives. A full grown turtle will reach three feet in length. They are most easily caught during the egg-laying season, when they are trapped on the sandy banks where they have gone to lay their eggs. The latter are greedily eaten, so that it is a wonder the species does not become extinct.

The birds of this valley are brilliant in their plumage beyond those of any other portion of the world. Parrots and paroquets of all sorts abound in countless numbers, some of the former being of large size. The finest species is the hyacinthine macaw, which is three feet long from the beak to the tip of its tail. With its beak this bird can crack a nut which is difficult to crack with a hammer. The toucan, with its curved beak almost as large as its body, the curious umbrella bird, the dancing "cock of the rock," the humming-birds and many other species add bright flashes of colour to the otherwise sombre colours of the woods.

It is in the numbers and varieties of insectivorous birds that these forests specially abound. Hundreds of them may be seen at almost any time moving about with the greatest activity, from species no larger than a sparrow to others the size of a crow. There are tanagers, ant-thrushes, fly-catchers and bargets, running up the trees and flitting about the leaves or lower branches. The hustling crowd lose no time, and, although seeming to move in concert, each bird is occupied on its own account in searching bark, leaf or twig. Then again, in a few minutes, all these hosts may disappear and the forest will remain deserted and silent. One bird, the organ bird, is a remarkable songster. When its notes are heard for the first time, it is hard to resist the impression that it is a human voice. It is especially noticeable because of the general absence of song birds in the tropical forests.

The numbers and varieties of insects are countless from the gorgeous butterflies to the leaf insects, which it is almost impossible for the uninitiated to discover because of the close resemblance to the foliage which they inhabit. The Amazon is really the despair of the naturalist by reason of the abundance of its plant and animal life. One naturalist reports having found upwards of seven thousand insects in one locality. Included in this list were five hundred and fifty distinct specimens of the butterfly. No description can convey an adequate idea of the beauty and diversity in form of this class of insects. There are many beautifully coloured beetles, whose delicate tints are marvels of beauty. There are flies which swarm along the banks in such numbers as to look like columns of smoke. The ants themselves are an interesting study, for their numbers are legion. There are ants that fly and ants that crawl; some that bite and others that sting; species that are carnivorous and species that are purely vegetable feeders; good and bad, big and little, industrious and lazy. No form of insect life is more interesting than these little creatures that can teach lessons to the human race. The jaguar, or tapir, does not create so great a commotion in the forest, as the armies of foraging ants which oftentimes march. They carry death and destruction to all other forms of insect life which can not fly far enough, or run fast enough, to escape these enemies. Wherever they move the whole animal world is set in commotion, and every living creature is possessed of but one idea, and that to get out of the way just as soon as possible. The ants march along in solid columns in a given direction, clearing the ground, bushes and small trees of every living thing. They will even attack a human being, if he should fail to get out of the way, and a few bites or stings will soon cause him to scamper away as fast as his legs can carry him.

A SCENE ON THE AMAZON NEAR ITS MOUTH.

For more than a hundred miles before reaching the mouth of the Amazon its dirty current colours the otherwise blue waters of the Atlantic. Entering the delta by one of the numerous outlets, the steamer passes through channels which are surrounded on either side by islands covered with dense vegetation a hundred feet or more high, with a border of lilies and other aquatic plants. It is like a fairy garden, and the islands are peopled with a noisy population of monkeys and parrots. Occasionally, a huge snake may be exposed to view on the limb of a tree. There are many kinds of trees, from adolescent saplings, as big as your arm, to immense trunks many feet through. And what a variety of palms! There are little palms that branch out like fans and do not grow high. There are palms, loaded with cocoanuts, which lean out over the water's edge at a very pronounced angle. One species is armed with fearful spines, but bears an edible nut, while the cohune palm grows great clusters of hard, oily nuts. Above all the members of this arborial family tower the lofty royal palms, which are the aristocrats of this family.

The native finds this tropical tree most useful, for

"To him the palm is a gift divine,
Wherein all uses of man combine,
House and raiment and food and wine."

The tree which bears the Brazil nuts of commerce is one of the highest of the Amazonian trees and overtops the royal palm. Its foliage is of a deep green and spreads out on all sides. The nuts grow in a great pod as large as a good-sized apple, and inside the thick husk will be found fifteen or twenty of these rich and delicious nuts. Flowering trees are omnipresent in these forests, and some of them are covered with beautiful flowers; or perhaps it may be a vine that bears the flowers one sees in the canopy overhead. They are neither buttercups nor violets, and yet it may be that they resemble those better known blossoms.

After threading this system of narrow channels the boat enters the river proper, which at first is very wide and is more like an inland sea; the natives call it the sea-river. In places it opens out in sea-like expanses; at times the boat coasts along the shore near enough to hear the monkeys chatter, and again it is out so far that the shore is only a hazy line. The lower river varies from two to ten miles in width, but you are never sure whether you are not mistaking the shores of islands for the actual banks of the river. Slowly past you floats débris that has come for two thousand miles on these yellow waters. Mixed up with the water may be soil from Peru, Ecuador, Bolivia and half of the republics of South America. You pass the mouths of streams which are themselves navigable for a thousand miles by vessels. In all it has been said that the Amazon and its tributaries furnish fifty thousand miles of navigable waters, half of which are available for steamers. There are few towns of any size, and only a few miserable little villages. Along the bank is an occasional cleared patch on which stands the little wood and thatch hut of a rubber gatherer. Naked babies play on the shores and barefooted men and women gaze at your steamer as it goes by. There are no roads in the forest, and if a path is blazed to-day in six months it would be impassable. Every one travels by water, except the rubber gatherers and medicine hunters, who chop their way through the undergrowth.

Nature's apothecary shop is located here, for hundreds of medicinal plants have been found in these woods and jungles. Sarsaparilla is probably the most profitable, but ipecac, oil of copaiba, and many other drugs useful in stopping a tooth-ache or poisoning a dog, are extracted from trees and vines of the Amazon Valley. Gums and balsams, essential oils and dyeing substances, spices and aromatic plants are also among the varied products.

Rain! Rain! Rain! One tires of hearing its ceaseless patter on the roof, and everything is soon covered with a coat of rust. Every article made of leather, which is allowed to stand for a few days, becomes covered with a down-like fungi of green mould. From November to February is the "rainy" season, and then the rain falls in perfect torrents, and the Amazon, fed by all its connecting streams, rises twenty-five, thirty or forty feet above its usual level. Thousands of square miles of territory are then submerged, and inland seas are formed in many places. The fall of the river is not more than two hundred inches in the first thousand miles from its mouth, and the current is not very swift. For this distance the depth will average one hundred and fifty feet.

After travelling up the Amazon as far as from Boston to Chicago the Rio Negro is reached. The name means the black river. As one writer says, "the Rio Negro is as black as one's hat and the Amazon is as yellow as pea soup." It is a very wide river at its mouth, and the steamer turns up into its black waters. Just ahead may be seen a haze of white buildings with their red tile roofs. Here, in the midst of this vast wilderness, where the forest stretches out for hundreds of miles in each direction, and where a monkey could travel for days by jumping from branch to branch, is located a live, hustling town with fine public buildings, electric lights, electric tram lines and a theatre that would be a credit to any town. The ridges of the roofs are sometimes so covered with turkey-buzzards as almost to make one think at first sight that they are artificial ornaments. They used to be the chief sanitary force, but the new waterworks and sewer system have greatly relieved their labours. Like Pará, this city smells of rubber and the day dreams of the inhabitants are permeated with that one idea.

Above the junction with the Rio Negro the Amazon is called the Solimoes, for a thousand miles, and beyond that it is known as the Marañon. At Iquitos, in Peru, this river is a mile wide. The area of the basin of this river is three times that of the Mississippi. The Tocantins, Xingu, Tapajos, Purus, Negro, Jurua, and Madeira, all noble streams in themselves, pour their floods into this one channel. The last named river leads to the famous Acre territory, which has proven a bonanza for Brazil. She paid

Bolivia $9,600,000 in 1904, and in the next five years it paid back nearly $24,000,000 in export duties on rubber alone.

The great traveller of a century ago, Baron von Humboldt, declared that "The valley of the Amazon in the near future is bound to become a great centre of civilization and the world's greatest storehouse." This prediction has not proven true, for more than a century has passed since the statement was made and little development has been made. The natural resources are there, just as Humboldt saw them, however, and still await the efforts of man to turn them to good account. Right at the mouth of the Amazon lies the great state of Pará, as large as two states the size of Texas, with only half a million inhabitants, less than one person to each square mile of territory, scattered over its confines. It has a fertile soil capable of producing almost anything necessary for the support and comfort of life; it possesses tablelands at an elevation high enough to escape the moisture of the river and continued heat of a tropical sun; in the mouth of the Amazon is an island almost as large as Portugal, which is capable of supplying thousands of head of cattle for the world's food supply.

The trouble with Pará is that the people think of nothing, deal in nothing and dream of nothing but rubber. To quote the American Consul: "Last year the United States took twenty thousand tons of crude rubber at a cost of $64,000,000, and we are still howling for more. The other things we took are small, although Brazil nuts, balsams, deerskins and a few other items amounted to something. What did we send them? Practically nothing that they could buy elsewhere. Some flour, petroleum, hardware and such other things as they themselves have looked up and found good." And yet the city of Pará is a thousand miles nearer to New York than it is to London or Hamburg, where the principal buying is done. The federal government receives twenty per cent. of the market value of every ton of rubber shipped, and in return promises, at some time in the future, to give the people good roads and other improvements. That happy day has not yet arrived, but rubber seems to be becoming higher each year and more difficult to procure. This perhaps accounts for the lack of improvement in some directions, that neither government nor people take time to think of anything except the one staple of rubber.

The city of Santa Maria de Belem do Pará is the principal port of the Amazon basin, and the greatest rubber shipping port in the world. It lies nearly a hundred miles from the Atlantic, but is as much on the Atlantic as New Orleans is on the Gulf, and is usually called an Atlantic port. It is only a few miles from the equator, and consequently is quite hot, for its elevation is only a few feet above sea level. And yet right here, almost on the "line," has grown up a beautiful city of over one hundred thousand people, who enjoy life and live almost as many years as those in more favourable locations. This city with the long name is generally known as Pará, although Belem, meaning Bethlehem, is the proper name. It is perhaps the prettiest city in Brazil, except Rio de Janeiro, and has many parks and plazas filled with the luxuriant vegetation and noble palms which grow so luxuriantly here. Statues ornament nearly all of their public squares and parks, and many of them are well done. The public buildings are numerous and tasty, as is most of the architecture of the country.

The sanitary conditions of the city have been greatly improved in the past few years, and a new sewer system to be worked by pumps something like the New Orleans method has just been begun. It is as a shipping port that the city is best known. To quote again from the American Consul: "Eight hundred and fifty-three steamers entered the port of Pará in 1908, having a tonnage of nine hundred and fifty thousand tons, but it was mainly remarkable for the fact that we did not fly the flag on even one cargo boat." It is only in the last few decades that this city has become very important, for no longer ago than the Civil War Pará was only a tropical trading port.

The docks are busy places, for steamers from all parts of the world, and flying many flags, come here. Men of all shades, from a dirty yellow to black and white, are busy handling the staple commodity of rubber. The rubber is all put up in sacks, and taken to the shipping houses, of which there are scores near the wharves. Every one handles "caoutchouc" and the air smells of it, the hot sun giving it an odour of burnt rubber. Everywhere they are cutting the dried rubber, which looks like great cheeses, chopping it, packing it, carrying it and loading it on vessels.

The Amazon district dominates the rubber market of the world. Pará and Manaos are the greatest rubber exporting ports of that district. From these cities the rubber buyers make their expeditions into the very heart of the Amazon, and its many tributaries are nearly all the home of rubber gatherers. From these centres the Indian gatherers make their expeditions by canoe, and through almost trackless forests to the trees which they are tapping. These trees do not grow in clumps, but one will be found here, another there, and oftentimes these single trees are at a distance of several hundred yards from each other. The amount of crude rubber that the native can gather depends on how close the trees may be to each other.

Upwards of one hundred rubber-bearing trees, vines and shrubs have been classified; but the one known as the *Hevea* is the rubber tree *par excellence* of Brazil. It is indigenous to the Amazon and its tributaries. Trees are oftentimes found which are as much as twelve feet in circumference, but those are exceptional. They require an abundance of moisture, and it is only in the thick forest, where the necessary moisture is constant and abundant, that they will reach this extraordinary size, although the trees can be successfully cultivated. It is quite probable that thousands of these trees are still undiscovered, and perhaps large districts still await development; but it is equally certain that the rubber prospector has threaded his way through thousands of miles of Amazonian jungle in his search after this profitable article of commerce. The present unprecedented prices have bestirred the exporting firms to feverish activity. Sections of hitherto unpierced forest are now being treaded by the prospector, with his Indian guides busily engaged in cutting a path through the dense undergrowth and labyrinth of vines. The howling of the enraged beasts thus disturbed in their lairs, the fear of poisonous snakes, the dread of the fever-laden mosquito, the annoyance of troublesome insects are nothing, with the price of rubber soaring upwards towards three dollars per pound.

An American rubber expert, who recently visited the Amazon rubber camps, says: "The past year more than seventy thousand tons of crude rubber, having a value approximating $300,000,000, were produced, of which forty thousand tons came out of the Amazon River. This was wholly wild rubber, gathered almost entirely from a belt extending along the Amazon and its tributaries, and running less than three miles into the interior. The vast forest beyond these borders is substantially untouched; but with the building of the railroad around the falls of the Madeira, which will be completed in 1911, with the building of roads through the forest connecting up rivers, and with the introduction of the gasoline boat, vast districts heretofore inaccessible will be brought within the reach of the rubber gatherer; and, while the gain in production each year has been approximately but ten per cent. over the previous year, there is no question that this percentage will increase largely from this time forward."

It is not the sap of the tree that produces the rubber, but a juice which is yielded by the bark. As it flows this juice has the appearance of milk, and acts in much the same way. If left to itself it will separate into a lower fluid and a surface mass like cream, and this is the so-called india-rubber. Less than fifteen per cent. of this "cream" in the product of the tree is unprofitable and does not pay for the working. Various ways have been devised to separate the rubber by processes of coagulation. The native method has always been by a smoking heat, but in some places chemicals are used; again separators, similar to those employed in butter making, have been introduced with good results, so it is said. The method and care used has a very marked influence on the price and value of the crude rubber in the markets. The heating by smoke is generally considered to produce the cleanest and purest form of rubber for commercial export.

The tapping of a rubber tree is a seemingly simple operation, and yet it requires considerable skill to so tap a tree as to produce the maximum of sap, and inflict the minimum of injury to the tree. A tree properly treated will stand continual tapping for twenty years, while a tree abused might die after two or three seasons. Hence it is to the interest of all to preserve the life of the tree. The tapper first affixes a small cup to the tree, and then with a wedge-shaped axe makes a gash in the bark, being careful not to penetrate the wood. This operation is repeated at intervals of a foot in a line around the tree. Into these cups the milk flows slowly. The next day a row of incisions is made just below the first, and so on until the ground is reached. A good tree will yield up to a height of at least twenty feet. An expert can tap a hundred trees a day, provided that they are close together. The sap, which is collected once each day, is then brought to the camp. Heat is then applied and the crude rubber is made into roughly-shaped balls of different sizes. The buyers usually cut these in two in order to see that no extraneous substance has been placed inside to give weight. Stones have frequently been found moulded in with the rubber, and stones are easier to gather even along the Amazon than rubber. Many plantations of rubber trees, principally of the Maniçoba species, which will grow on higher and drier lands of the interior, have been set out in Brazil, but their production is very small when compared with that of the dense Amazonian forests.

Of the other valuable trees of the Amazon basin Agassiz says: "The importance of the basin of the Amazons to Brazil, from an industrial point of view, can hardly be over-estimated. Its woods alone have an almost priceless value. Nowhere in the world is there finer timber, either for solid construction or for work of ornament, and yet it is scarcely used even for the local buildings, and makes no part whatever of the exports. The rivers which flow past these magnificent forests seem meant to serve, first as a waterpower for the sawmills, which ought to be established along their borders, and then as a means of transportation for the material so provided. Setting aside the woods as timber, what shall I say of the mass of fruits, resins, oils, colouring matters and textile fabrics which they yield?" These words of this great naturalist, although written years ago, are just as true to-day. At least one hundred and fifty varieties of valuable hardwood timbers have been found in these forests. As mahogany and other better known woods become scarcer, these woods will certainly find a market.

A NEW SETTLER IN THE JUNGLE.

The great state of Amazonas, which is more than two-thirds as large as the United States east of the Mississippi, is an empire in itself. It is difficult to predict what may be its future. Some scientific men say that civilization will again be centred in the tropics; if so, then here will be the future Europe. Any prediction would be only guesswork, for no man with only human foresight could look into the future and foretell the development. The possibilities are visible to even the shallow observer; the uncertain trend of civilization no one can with certainty prognosticate. Nature is kind, if her laws are obeyed, and the white man endures the climate better than his copper-coloured brother. It would be the lazy man's paradise, for it takes little labour to provide the simple wants. The only difficult task is to fight nature in her prodigal growth. The struggle of the northern farmer with weeds is an infantile task in comparison with the constant fight against every kind of growth in this climate. It would be a hopeless task for one man, lone handed and without means, to locate in this wilderness and attempt to carve out his fortune. Goodly sized colonies would do better, and, by their energetic and united efforts, nature would be conquered and compelled to contribute of her bounty to the welfare and support of man.

Outside of Manaos and a few small towns and settlements the population of the state of Amazonas consists almost entirely of Indians. One industrious writer has listed nearly four hundred separate and distinct tribes. Many of these are extinct, or practically extinct, but a large number of distinct tribes are still found on the different rivers that have widely divergent habits and physical characteristics. A few of these tribes live a retired existence in the forests, but most of them mingle with the white people, and are employed by them in gathering rubber or other products of the forests. The skin of the Indians is a coppery-brown colour. They are of a medium height, but have not the high cheek bones of the North American Indian. Like the latter, however, they are undemonstrative, and do not betray their emotions of joy and grief, wonder or fear. They will undoubtedly be driven out and disappear as the white race settle in the tropics, for their inflexible character prevents them from adapting themselves to changed conditions.

Although these Indians have dropped cannibalism, and other inhuman practices, they are still simple children in their customs and beliefs. They live as their ancestors have lived for centuries, have adopted few of the conveniences or luxuries of civilization, and live a hand-to-mouth existence. Religious holidays are observed with a strange mixture of superstition. Their idea of a holiday, whether religious or secular, is "bonfires, processions, masquerading, confused drumming and fifing, monotonous dancing kept up hour after hour without intermission, and, the most important part of all, getting gradually and completely drunk." They are kindly disposed toward aliens, and are as hospitable as their circumstances permit. The Tupi-Guarini language is generally spoken, or at least understood, and this has been reduced to written form by the Jesuit clergy.

CHAPTER X
THE PEOPLE AND THEIR CHARACTERISTICS

The Brazilian people are made up of three distinct races: Europeans of every nationality, but most of Latin origin, Indians and negroes, the latter two nationalities being more or less mixed in the process of assimilation, and distributed all along the seaboard and the rivers, from the Amazon to the Paraná. In Brazil there is no race problem or antagonism between white and black, or Indian, and the hopeful ones say that in course of time not only all race distinctions, but even colour distinction, will disappear, and be merged in the new Brazilian type.

The pure Indians are now found only on the Amazon, the headwaters of the Paraguay, and the sections remote from the railways of such states as São Paulo, Paraná, Bahia and others. Most of them were never the bloodthirsty race that our own redskins were, although a number of the tribes were cannibalistic in their practices. The number still existing is placed at about six hundred thousand. There was no regular spreading of civilization and population, but it was done through the sporadic settlement of advancing posts which were pushed out into the wilderness. They were at first armed against the Indians, who were then hostile, but most of the aborigines were finally subjugated, and gathered into settlements by the conquerors. These settlements formed the nuclei about which the towns began to grow. As there were few European women in the country, the Portuguese took wives from among the conquered people, and such a connection was not considered a *mesalliance*, even by those of good birth.

From these alliances arose the mixture of Indians and Europeans, which runs through many of the very best families in Brazil. In the state of São Paulo, for instance, this mixture became very marked, and produced an almost white race as the strain of Indian blood became less. It was from this race that the original "Paulistas" sprang, who distinguished themselves among the Brazilians for their bravery in driving the savage Indians from the coast, and later by their enterprise and administrative capacity. I met one of these men in that state who was a wealthy *fazendero*, and a graduate of one of the best schools in our own land. I was impressed by his courtesy and intelligence, and finally asked him from what nationality he was descended. He said that his ancestry were Portuguese and Indian. "And," he then added, "I am proud of the Indian blood in me." From the way he said it, it was plain to be seen that he meant it; and such is the feeling of all those who have that mixture. Some of the very best men in that and other states have at least a slight trace of the aborigine blood in their veins.

NEGROES IN BRAZIL.

The negroes, just as in our own land, were originally brought to Brazil and sold in bondage. The first slaves were imported into the state of Bahia in 1574. Just seventeen years later the official records give the population of that settlement as two thousand whites, four thousand negro slaves and six thousand civilized Indians. This will give a little idea of how rapidly the negroes were brought into the country by the slave traders. Great sugar plantations were worked, and on these were employed the cheap labour. The black slaves so exceeded in number the whites that insurrections broke out in many places. In Minas Geraes, for instance, out of a population of fifty thousand in the early part of the eighteenth century, thirty-five thousand were negro slaves, and most of these recent imports. Some of the whites were so fearful of their own lives, that the governor petitioned the King to put into execution the "Black Code," which meant that the right leg of a fugitive slave might be cut off and a wooden one substituted. Thus, by terror, the excess of blacks was kept in subjection.

The proportion of black population is much greater in the northeastern states than elsewhere. As one journeys south they become less numerous, until, when you reach the extreme southern states, they are uncommon. In the state of Bahia, those with a negro admixture far outnumbered the whites. This is due not only to the fact that slavery was first introduced there, but also because it was sooner abolished in that state, and fugitive slaves escaping from the coffee plantations fled there, just as they did to our own Northern states. Those who were able to buy their freedom in other states went there as well as those who were voluntarily freed by their masters, as thousands were all over Brazil. In Minas Geraes perhaps one-third of the population have negro blood in their veins.

When slavery was finally abolished, in 1888, there were perhaps seven hundred and fifty thousand slaves in the empire, the most of these being held in the coffee producing states. In São Paulo to-day the negro population is very small, as it is said that the former slaves soon became decimated by the excesses in which they indulged when freedom was gained. In the whole republic perhaps very near to one-half the entire population has at least a trace of negro blood in their veins. The mixture is very marked in the north, and down as far as Rio de Janeiro, and almost to São Paulo. There is, however, no race prejudice that I could perceive. In schools I saw kinky-haired boys and girls side by side with the whites, and in all public places they mingled freely. Negro lawyers and doctors appeared to be patronized by the whites, and their families seemed to have friends among all classes. Officially, at least, there is no distinction, and men have occupied the highest offices in the republic, who unmistakably had a trace of the negro blood. Americans, who live there, as well as some native Brazilians, tell me that there is a growing prejudice among those free from the negro blood against that race, and even the slightest mixture of it, until it has now become very noticeable in many ways, and is even making itself felt in political circles. I am making this statement solely upon the authority of those who live there, and ought to know better than a traveller; but, as for myself, I saw no evidence whatever of such a state of public sentiment.

Says Dr. Hale in his book, "The South Americans," "I was invited one evening to a small dinner-party at which we were to meet Senhorita X——, a young lady freshly launched into society, whose musical talent was exceptional, even in this land naturally so gifted with love of both poetry and music. I was the only one of the guests who had not met her, so that she was smothered with greetings before I was presented; but when my turn came, I was astonished to find before me what we would call a mulatto—kinky hair, thick lips and prominent teeth. There was not the least trace of embarrassment in her or the rest of the company. She sat opposite me at table, played for us later some brilliant piano pieces, and kissed all the ladies good-bye with so much ease that was absolutely impossible to conceive any difference among us on account of race."

The next largest foreign element is the Italian, of whom there are two million or more. They readily adapt themselves to Brazil, because of the similarity of customs and language. They are frugal and industrious, and are gradually acquiring wealth and power. A great influence has also been wielded by the German colonists who flocked to Southern Brazil in great numbers, about the middle of last century. There are perhaps nearly one-half million of this stock. They have not progressed as have the Germans in the United States, perhaps because a living came too easily, and nature was too bountiful. The majority of them went to Brazil after the revolution of 1848, and one can trace many of the settlements by the names of the towns. They do not intermingle or intermarry with the Brazilians like the other colonists, and one can find whole communities where no one understands the Portuguese language. They are citizens of Brazil, and yet take little interest in the body politic, neither caring for the position of alderman or policeman.

It is the Portuguese element in Brazil, of course, that are the most interesting, and there is at least a remnant of the pure Portuguese left. And they have many good and excellent qualities. As a race they frequently lack what Americans term the practical element, but they have some of the finer traits, frequently missing in our own people. They have an innate courtesy which is sometimes almost overwhelming. If the same thing was done by an Anglo-Saxon, in the same profuse manner, it would be looked upon as overdone; but, coming from a Brazilian, it is done with such a grace and smoothness that seems only natural. You are greeted with an exquisite courtesy, especially after one or two meetings, and the parting is a series of courtesies. You shake hands about half a dozen times before finally separating, then pause and turn as you reach the door and make a final bow before leaving the room; and this final courtesy is always awaited by your host. If friends separate, or meet after an absence, they fall into one another's arms and mutually pat each other on the back as a mark of affection. This is never done upon first acquaintance. It is a slow ceremony when there is a large list to be greeted, but it is faithfully gone through with; first a hand shake, and then the embrace if the intimacy warrants it.

The street car conductor hands you your ticket with a little courtesy, and even the hotel servant, and they are always men, finds time to say *obligado* (much obliged), when you hand him the gratuity he expects as a matter of right. The *carigador* at the station, who carries your baggage to the train, may haggle with you over the price, but when the affair is settled he courteously tips his hat and wishes you a *bom viaje*, which means "a pleasant voyage." If you remove your coat on the train, or enter a first-class car without wearing a collar and tie, the conductor reproves you with a little courtesy, as though he was performing a very unpleasant duty. The clerk in the store never hurries you in making your purchases, but patiently places himself at your disposition. And so it is as you travel all through the country, there is courtesy present everywhere, and you can not help but like the people for these traits.

LABOURERS' HOMES ON A PLANTATION.

They might also teach us something in their philosophical outlook upon life. The doctrine of "don't hurry" and "don't worry" is deeply rooted, and gives them greater enjoyment in life than among a race whose nerves are continually on edge. They resent any assumption of superiority, but recognize freely and generously the good qualities of the Anglo-Saxon. There is a lax moral tone on the part of the men which could be much improved, and which would greatly benefit the country at large.

In the homes that I visited excellent taste was shown in the furnishing and decorations. There was only one arrangement that grew painfully monotonous. In the reception room a couch was always placed against the wall, and the chairs for guests invariably placed at right angles to this, a row at each end. This gives the host or hostess a chance to see each guest, and the favoured one is invited to share it with her, or possibly to occupy it alone. The chairs are oftentimes stiff and uncomfortable, but it is bad taste to move them, or twist around in them, as Americans are often accustomed to do. The house is yours for the time being. As one man told me in broken English, "your house" and "your friend." And it was my house, at least I was welcome in it; and he was my friend, I am pleased to say, for he proved it. When you are going away in Brazil, your friends always accompany you to the station, no matter how far away or how early in the morning. I must admit it is a pretty custom, and makes you feel that friends are a good thing to have. I have had Brazilian friends, of only a few days' standing, perform this little courtesy, men of prominence and influence, and I confess that it reaches a tender place in my heart.

The Brazilian women are handsome in their youth. Their bright eyes and dark features at that age are very fascinating. Especially in Rio their physique is much better than that of the men, for the "stronger sex" in that city are mostly narrow-shouldered and rather thin-chested. The women dress with good taste, but their styles have no uniqueness about them, for they wear the same high-heeled, uncomfortable-looking shoes, and the same large Parisian-shaped hats that have driven men to despair the world over. As their years increase, however, they have a tendency to become stout, due perhaps to hearty eating and lack of exercise. I must say that the Brazilians are particularly fond of eating, and in this hot climate will devour much more food, and especially meat, than those from colder climes; and, in addition, they seldom eat the noon breakfast, or dinner, without at least half a bottle of light wine of some kind.

At Rio, and in Northern Brazil, the women are subject to all the social restrictions that have ever been the lot of women in Latin countries. The young women can not go out unaccompanied by an older woman or the family servant, and in the social life there is nothing of what American women would term freedom. They perhaps do not miss this so much, for it has been the custom of the race for generations untold. At São Paulo, and some of the other southern states, there is a noticeable breaking away from the centuries-old traditions, due, perhaps, to foreign influence. There one can see even young Brazilian ladies out alone on a shopping tour; and, although there is not freedom of association among young people of the two sexes, the beginning of the change is apparent, and I would not be surprised to see even a radical change in this respect in another decade or two. The women there are beginning to feel the narrowness of their lives, and to long for the freedom which they see the young people of other nationalities enjoy. One will likewise find women employed in some of the stores, and occasionally, in other public positions in the cities of that state.

It is true that political ideals in Brazil are not so lofty as they should be. If the reports of investigation committees are true in our own land, however, our own stables need a little looking after. There is undoubtedly more "graft" in Brazil than with us. Nevertheless, the Brazilians are not without ideals. The development of the artistic in parks and buildings is a convincing proof of this. The officials demand work to be up to specifications, and then want their "graft" to be over and above this, instead of the American practice of "skinning the job" to accomplish the same end. This is their system, and there is generally not so much coarse juggling as sometimes happens with us. Bankruptcy is not so common as with us, and bills contracted by private individuals are generally paid. The men are reprehensible in their private conduct, but the women are generally good.

Said an American to me, who has lived in that country for forty years, and who is the best judge of Brazilian character that I know: "The Brazilian women, those who have not the mixture of negro blood, are good and pure, and in them lie the great hope of the race." They are domestic, are the mothers of large families, and nowhere is there a sincerer love for their children shown than by these Brazilian women. In Rio there is a fast set, just as there is in every large city where there is wealth, and an idle class, and where every opportunity exists for the indulgence in vice. In the lower classes, and there are practically only two classes in Brazil, looseness in the sexual relation is very common and the percentage of illegitimacy is high. It is not looked down upon, and neither the unfortunate children nor their mothers receive social ostracism.

The upper classes of the Brazilians are a well educated and cultivated people. Most of them have been schooled in France, and speak the French language almost as fluently as their own. In Paris there is always a goodly sized Brazilian colony, and the boats passing between Rio and Europe always carry a number of Brazilians to and from that European capital. They find the atmosphere of the French capital more congenial, and full of the *simpatica* which means so much to the Latin people. The girls who go abroad for education are all sent to the convents of France, but many boys are now sent to schools in the States, especially for a technical education. Those who do go come back enthusiastic over the United States, and many of them bring back American wives, much to the discomfiture of the parents.

An aristocracy exists which can yet be traced, and it is an aristocracy of wealth. It divides, with a sharp distinction, the aristocracy from the labouring element. It is perhaps unreasonable to expect the classes developed by a monarchical form of government to disappear so soon, for the spirit was imbued in the dozen or more generations preceding the present one. Among that class it was considered a disgrace to labour with one's hands, and this fact has made politics and the holding of political positions a profession. This weakness in politics is, in my opinion, one of the evils of Brazil. It becomes a business and a passion with the men, even in a more intense degree than in our own land. The young man must first secure the title of doctor, and every professional man, physician, lawyer, civil engineer, teacher, etc., receives this title.[1] Then he must obtain some government appointment. Finally, when his own prestige becomes great enough, he seeks election to some office. To politics can be blamed the lack of advancement in many lines.

Said one of the wealthiest and most progressive business men in Rio de Janeiro, himself a Brazilian, to me: "Politics are the curse of the country. It is all words and delay. The politicians like to talk about their great country. They boast that the Amazon is the greatest river in the world, so large that the Mississippi dwindles into an insignificant stream in comparison; that Rio is the finest harbour in the world and capable of floating all the navies in existence; and that Brazil has the greatest undeveloped natural resources in the world. When any of the resources are developed, however, it is not these men who help to do it, but it is the foreigner who sees the opportunity and grasps it. Congress meets and talks politics, instead of passing the necessary legislation. They want to subsidize everything instead of giving competition a chance. I am past sixty years of age, and it has been that way ever since I can remember." This is quite a severe arraignment of the evils of politics, but it was exemplified during my own visit. The regular session of Congress came to an end in October, and a special session was at once convened, because the necessary appropriation bills had not been passed. This was just a few days before the special service must adjourn, and no progress had then been made. Long speeches were made, but most of the talk was regarding the two candidates for the presidency. As this was the first time in the history of the country that there had been two active candidates for this high office, the senators and deputies spent their time arguing the merits of their respective candidates. The Congress had then been in continuous session for almost nine months.

Another unfortunate condition and characteristic is the dependence upon what Americans would term "pull," or influence. Even the well qualified young man depends more upon that than upon the real qualifications he possesses. So many are looking for "soft snaps" that it becomes absolutely necessary to provide them. I heard of this from so many sources, both native and foreign, that I am fully impressed with its evil. It is even customary in educational institutions for students, who have not been diligent, to bring to their professors at examination time letters of recommendation from influential persons, stating why this particular student should be passed or given his degree. Foreign teachers soon shut down upon this method, and it has had a beneficial effect in their schools. Any work that is done under a concession must have a government inspector on the payrolls, and the man appointed is frequently one who knows nothing about the work, but draws his salary. A college must have a government inspector, who has nothing in particular to do except that he must attend the examinations, and no degree is granted without his approval. This inspector may or may not be qualified for the position, but the salary of three hundred milreis per month from the college makes it a nice political appointment, for it is practically a sinecure.

The Brazilians are ambitious, but a lack of energy interferes with what they otherwise might accomplish. In many of the government departments and industries foreigners are employed at large salaries, which might just as well be filled by natives, if the young men would only qualify themselves. Very many of the agricultural schools and experimental stations are in the charge of foreigners, Americans, Belgians, French and German. They are rather fanciful and visionary in their plans, and will not begin at the bottom as is necessary. They would rather build the superstructure first, for that is the showy part. It is perhaps the innate ambition, however, that will finally lead the country out of the rut. They are willing to be led but cannot be driven.

"There is no public opinion in Brazil," said one of the most influential and ablest men in Brazil, a man who has travelled extensively and made a study of other nations. "The masses do not think. The politicians plan and carry out things themselves and create the opinion." This strikes me as being true. Politicians are the same everywhere, and here they have practically a free hand. A large percentage of the population are not able to read or write, and the percentage of those who do take an interest in politics is small. They say that there is no use; but it is a bad precedent. In every state there is a small clique who rule the politics of that state. If a man announces himself as a candidate for president, for instance, these wise men get together and announce their positions; and this announcement is everywhere taken without question, as the choice of the state. No political ring in the United States has ever been able to wield such absolutely despotic power as these cliques. There the voters will occasionally wake up and smash the corrupt machine, while in Brazil the elections are usually merely perfunctory occasions that must be gone through with. This does not mean that every one of these machines is bad, for many of the men who have this power use it for the benefit of the people, and have done much to advance the interests of the masses. To them great credit should be given, for, having it in their power to do absolutely as they wish, they have the courage and honesty to use this power in the interest of the people, just as much as if they had secured it from the people by a popular suffrage. Out of the eighteen million people in the country there are perhaps six hundred thousand qualified to vote, and there have never been more than four hundred thousand votes cast in any presidential election.

The people enjoy play, and always welcome *"festa"* occasions. Holidays are numerous and all join in their celebration. Brazil has two independence days, the 7th of September and the 15th of November, which are national holidays and universally celebrated. The carnival season, however, which occurs the week preceding Lent, is the occasion of the greatest merrymaking. It lasts for three whole days in Rio de Janeiro, and, during that time, business is wholly suspended in the cities. There are processions with music, and the streets are full of people in mask and gown, who dance and sing and blow horns and make disagreeable noises in general. Disguised in dominoes and masks they blow their horns, talk in falsetto voices, while the balconies and windows are filled with crowds of onlookers, women and children being especially prominent. Few people wear their best clothes, for it is the custom to squirt perfumed water over passers-by from these balconies. This perfumed water is contained in little leaden vials, which are sold at stands all over the city. The streets are hung with the banners of all nations, little flags and coloured lanterns, and have all the appearance of a gala occasion.

THE FIFTEENTH OF NOVEMBER IN SÃO PAULO.

On the last of the three days a grand procession is held. It is a procession of mounted military bands, men and women in ancient costume, immense floats, *papier-mache* figures, grotesque animal representations, men burlesquing women actresses, and women dressed as pages. King Carnival, upon a gorgeous throne, is always a part of the procession. The procession winds in and around one street after another, along the Avenida Central and the Beira Mar, and often takes hours to pass a given point. At night masquerade balls at the various theatres end the gaieties. The galleries and boxes are always filled with an interested audience, but the floor is given up to revelry and suggestive dancing, which would not merit the approval of polite society.

CHAPTER XI
EDUCATION AND THE ARTS

The educational facilities in Brazil are not of the best in the republic as a whole. In some of the states, such as São Paulo, Rio de Janeiro and a part of Minas Geraes, the provisions are fairly good, but in none of them has the work been systematized in the same way that it has in our own land. Until the establishment of the republic the instruction was almost entirely in the hands of the church, but the duty now rests upon the various states and municipalities. Statistics upon education in Brazil are very unreliable, just as are their census reports, so that whatever or whosesoever figures are followed there will be errors. It is perhaps safe to say that not over twenty-five per cent. of the total population are able to read and write.

The government has issued a volume which gives the figures of school enrolment of the various states, which is the first attempt on the part of the federal government to give educational statistics. In a few of the states, so the official report says, the estimates of school enrolment are not complete, since it was impossible to secure complete returns from some of the rural districts, but in the main they may serve to give a fairly adequate idea of the educational facilities in the republic; at any rate, they are the best figures that are obtainable. The figures include all schools, whether of public or private character, state or municipal. The total number of primary schools reported is eleven thousand one hundred and forty-seven, of which one thousand eight hundred and fifteen are public municipal schools, seven thousand and eighty nine public schools under state control, and mostly in the smaller towns and villages, and two thousand two hundred and forty-five private schools, most of which are in the larger towns and cities. The state schools, which are improperly designated as rural schools, have an enrolment of three hundred and forty thousand six hundred and ninety-seven, and an attendance of two hundred and forty thousand six hundred and ninety. The municipal schools have an enrolment of one hundred and six thousand seven hundred and fifty-four, and an attendance of sixty-nine thousand four hundred and thirty-two. Private primary schools have an enrolment of one hundred and ten thousand eight hundred and forty-one, and an attendance of eighty-one thousand and sixty-six. Of the three hundred and twenty-seven secondary institutions twenty-nine are public and two hundred and ninety-eight under private control, the former having an enrolment of four thousand and the latter of twenty-six thousand two hundred and fifty-eight. No figures of the actual attendance at these institutions were given, but it would probably not be much less than the enrolment. If these government figures are correct, and the population is twenty million five hundred and fifteen thousand as claimed, in that same report, then scarcely three per cent. of the population may be regarded as enjoying school privileges. This estimate takes on new significance when one considers that the proportion of rural population is very high, as compared with the entire population, and shows how much less the facilities are in those sections. In the Federal District, for instance, which includes the city of Rio de Janeiro, and where the population is almost entirely urban, there is an estimated population of eight hundred and fifty-eight thousand, and a school enrolment of sixty-one thousand nine hundred and thirty-three. In the state of Alagoas, on the other hand, with an almost equal population, and where it is altogether rural with the exception of a few coast towns, there is a school enrolment of only fourteen thousand and ninety-two. The state of Pernambuco, with only one town of any size, and that the capital, has a school enrolment of only twenty-two thousand eight hundred and fifty-two, in a reported population of one million three hundred and ten thousand. More comparisons might be made, but with these explanations the reader can figure them out from the table.[2]

A SCHOOL FOR BOYS IN SÃO PAULO.

The school instruction, except in the Federal District and the professional schools, is in the hands of the various states. In none of them does a compulsory educational law exist, and, if it did, the facilities do not exist to take care of those of school age who would thus be obliged to attend. As will be seen by the comparisons the provisions for instruction and the illiteracy vary much in the different states. Some of the states are richer than others, and can afford to spend more money for public requirements, and others are naturally more progressive. All of the schools in the various states are modelled on the same general plan. I have chosen those of São Paulo for illustration, because that state has made better progress along educational lines than the others, and because I made a special study of the school system of that state.

A SCHOOL FOR GIRLS IN SÃO PAULO.

The schools are divided into three classes: primary, secondary and superior. The primary schools are again divided into preliminary and complementary instruction. The preliminary instruction is given in ungraded schools, and the law requires the establishment of an ungraded school in every community where there are from twenty to forty pupils of school age, although this has not always been done. Where there are six or more of these schools, a "school group" may be established, in which teaching is graded. In this state there are about eighty of these school groups. In addition there are a number of night schools where similar instruction is given to those who are unable to attend the day schools, or who have passed the school age and lacked the opportunity for an education in their youthful days. Of these there are thirty-four in the state at the present time. A few free kindergarten schools are also maintained in the capital, but this feature of instruction has not been developed much as yet.

The secondary instruction is given in what are termed gymnasiums. All of these schools, whether public or private, in order to be recognized over the country, must conform to the regulations laid down by the National Gymnasium at Rio de Janeiro. They must observe the programmes and courses of study laid down by that institution, and the student in one of these gymnasiums is given the degree of bachelor of letters, or science, after a course of study covering six years. In the state of São Paulo, there are three of these schools: one in São Paulo, one in Campinas and one in Riberão Preto. The course of study is about equal to that of the average high school in the United States, and prepares the student to matriculate in the schools for superior instruction. The so-called superior schools are those devoted to technical and professional education. For superior instruction there are in this state two institutions: the Law School and the Polytechnic School, of which the former is a federal institution, and has graduated some of the brightest lawyers and statesmen of the republic. The Polytechnic School is devoted, as its name indicates, to the teaching of the practical sciences, and is fitted with the necessary apparatus for such instruction. The school year in the public schools is generally from the first of February, or March, to the end of the following November, but the professional schools do not begin as a rule until the first of April. A model school, the Braz *Grupo*, is maintained in São Paulo, which is used as the name would indicate, as an example for the other schools.

One school of which this state is very proud is the Normal School, which has departments for all grades from the kindergarten up. Its primary object is to prepare teachers for the work in the other schools, and in this respect it is doing an admirable work. As its accommodation is limited the students are only admitted upon special recommendation, and it is sometimes difficult for a boy or girl to secure admittance, as it is always full. The normal course extends over a period of four years, and covers a wide range of subjects. It is fitted up with a good library, a chemical laboratory, gymnasium, modelling rooms and apparatus for manual work. It has turned out several hundred graduates, of whom the proportion of women exceeds that of men in about the same proportion as they do in our own land.

The director of public instruction in this state is a progressive man, and is making many improvements in the work. He made a trip to the United States in order to study the system there, and brought back a great many practical ideas. He is arranging the courses of study and method of instruction in the schools of this state after the system in use in the United States. It cannot be done all at once as there are certain prejudices in the minds of some that must first be overcome. This process has been in operation for several years, and one can see the good results. The building was originally planned by an American lady teacher, who was brought down for that purpose. The only two modern languages taught, except the Portuguese, are French and English. This is a compliment to our tongue to have it chosen in preference to the German and Spanish, as is generally the rule. Their method of teaching the English is very practical too. This means that in the course of a few years the English language will be much more common than it is to-day. I found that the people were anxious to learn English, and those who did know it were proud of the accomplishment. Formerly they desired to know only French, in addition to Portuguese, for that was the polite language; but, as commerce has developed, the desire to know English has increased in proportion, until now all those who are able to go to the higher institutions of learning are taking up the study of English.

There are a number of other institutions of learning in this state, most of them under the auspices of the various Roman Catholic orders. Some of these schools are of a very high order and are doing their share in the work of raising the standard of education. One of the best of their institutions is a large convent school for the education of girls. The most important non-Catholic institution is the Mackenzie College, which was founded by Presbyterian missionaries, but is now undenominational. At its head is the venerable Dr. Horace M. Lane, a scholarly and able man, whom I am glad to enrol as a friend. Dr. Lane first came to Brazil in 1857 as a physician, and has lived there continuously since that time, except for a period of fourteen years, during which he practised medicine in the United States. When the college was endowed with $50,000 by John T. Mackenzie, of New York, whose name it now bears, Dr. Lane was chosen president and has remained at the head ever since. The will of the above benefactor left the college a large additional sum of money. Dr. Lane understands the Brazilians as few Americans do. He is a very kindly and generous critic, and frankly tells them their faults without flattery. His candour and frankness have won him friends and the respect of all, and even of the Catholic clergy. Mackenzie College is unique in that it has never asked recognition of the government, but is affiliated with the University of the State of New York. This institution has been in existence a number of years, and its instructors have had the pleasure of seeing many of its graduates reach positions of the greatest importance, both at home and abroad. The resident foreigners send their children there, and the Brazilians do likewise. A graduate of Mackenzie College has a recognized standing all over the republic even though it has not asked for government recognition, and placed itself under the necessity of maintaining an official inspector on its pay roll.

STUDENTS AT THE AGRICULTURAL COLLEGE, PIRACICABA.

The O Granberry College, at Juiz de Fora, in the state of Minas Geraes, is another progressive North American college, under the auspices of the Methodist Episcopal Church South, that is making a reputation in Brazil. I had the privilege of attending the commencement exercises at this college, in company with the American Ambassador and his military attaché. The *festa* exercises, as they term it in Brazil, were attended by a very large audience. Representative citizens of the community, including the mayor of the city and the president of the Camara, which is a sort of county council, were present on the platform. This shows a truly liberal spirit, for perhaps only a very small proportion of the audience were other than Roman Catholics. This school maintains, in addition to the regular academic courses, schools of pharmacy, dentistry and theology. Their schools of pharmacy and dentistry are among the very best in the republic. A government military instructor is also kept to drill the boys and young men in military tactics, much the same as in the colleges of our own land. I was surprised to find a number of young women taking up the study of pharmacy and dentistry, for it seemed a wide departure in this land of conservativeness and tradition, which has heretofore denied to woman that larger field granted to the sex in Anglo-Saxon countries. The generous spirit and encouragement shown to these institutions, conducted by aliens and Protestants, and the wider field granted to women, are good omens, I believe, for the future of the land.

A number of states have established agricultural schools, which promise much for the future. The best one of these schools is the Escola Agricola, at Piracicaba, which is maintained by the state of São Paulo. The site for this college was presented to the state by one of its progressive citizens. The Secretary of Agriculture of that state travelled widely throughout the United States and Europe, studying places and methods, and finally decided to establish the school on the American system. He then engaged Dr. Clinton D. Smith, an American, who had been at the head of a prominent agricultural college in the United States, to take charge of the work. The faculty also include two Frenchmen, one Belgian, one Bulgarian, one Portuguese and a number of Brazilians, making quite a cosmopolitan board of instructors.

The institution is housed in a large, beautiful building, and its equipment is equal to our own best institutions. The student is instructed in the analysis of soils, and the introduction of modern machinery for their cultivation; in botany, and a good course in stock raising; and in physics, even to measuring the force of a waterfall, or winding a dynamo. There is also a course in physiology, hygiene and medicine for emergencies, as well as much-needed instruction in political economy. The most practical feature is the actual work on the farm which every student is obliged to do. He must work for two hours each day in the actual occupation of handling a plow, rigging a harrow, managing a mower or reaper, and learn how to repair any of the common machines on the plantation. Students from a number of states attend the school, and many of them are sons of wealthy Brazilians. As the able director told me: "It is a good and much-needed training for a set of boys born where slavery was in existence, and in a land where to work with the hands is a sign of inferiority. The hope of the college is to exert a fundamental influence on agriculture, where monoculture is the rule and polyculture ought to be." It will do more than that, for such instruction will have an important bearing in developing the character of these young men as well.

Portuguese writers are prolific. Few countries have produced more literature, compared with the number who speak the language, than Portugal and Brazil. The Portuguese language is especially rich in expression, and is said to be the nearest to the classic Latin of any living dialect. It lends itself easily to poetic expression, and there have been many poets. The Brazilians are fond of elaborate and flowery expressions, and this verboseness and ornate form of expression runs through their literature and public speaking. At the commencement exercises mentioned above the addresses of some of the graduates were most elaborate. Where an American graduate would have started out with "Ladies and Gentlemen," and perhaps have added "our dear professors and honourable trustees," the Brazilian youth took several minutes to make his introductory remarks, and pass around his compliments to the professors and other dignitaries who were on the stage. No one was omitted in the general round of compliments. Impromptu poems spring up on every and all occasions, and the recent visit of a high state official of the United States prompted more than one poetic effusion, many of which were fortunately suppressed by the committees in charge of the festivities.

Brazil has produced a number of eminent writers. The best known, and perhaps most widely loved of all, is Gonçalves Diaz, who has been called the Longfellow of Brazil. He died nearly a half century ago, but his memory has been honoured by monuments and streets named in his honour, and his name has been kept green by continuous quotations from his writings. The "Song of the Exile," written by him, has been called the "Home, Sweet Home" of the Brazilians, and is said to be quoted more than any other poem in the language. Says Mrs. Wright:[3] "No translation has ever been made which in any sense reveals the exquisite delicacy of touch in the original, or its plaintive rhythmic melody, though many attempts have been made to put it into English and other languages. Throughout the six stanzas of which it is composed, the little poem voices a heart cry of homesickness. After recounting, with childlike simplicity, the charm of his native land, its palm trees, and the sweet-voiced Sabiá, the favourite songbird of Brazil, he prays with touching pathos to be spared to return, that he may once more see its glorious palms and hear the Sabiá sing." Diaz had received a good education in Portugal, and became a professor of history in the college at Rio. Many of his poems have a historic basis and deal with events of history. He served on several government commissions, among which was a trip up the Amazon with a scientific commission. On this trip his health was ruined, and from that time he was an invalid to the time of his death. On his return from a trip to Europe his vessel was shipwrecked, and his remains went to a watery grave, at the early age of forty.

There have been many other and excellent writers, both of fiction and poetry, in the past century, but few of them are known to the English-speaking world, as translations have not been made. Some excellent histories have been written also, which have been fostered and preserved by the Brazilian Historical and Geographical Institute. Dr. Machado de Assis is one of the most distinguished living writers, who has written both poetry and fiction. Dr. Olavo Bilac has also written many beautiful poems, and is one of the best-known writers and orators of the day. I had the pleasure of meeting him, and listening to an address by him, and it was a very pleasing address, distinguished for its purity of style. Dr. Ruy Barbosa, prominent also in political circles, has been a prolific writer in many lines. There is scarcely an important subject that his pen has not touched upon, from fiction to the intricate problem of international law. Baron de Rio Branco, a member for many years of the official cabinet, and Dr. Joaquim Nabuco, late Ambassador to the United States, who died a few months ago in Washington, are also writers of considerable merit.

The press of Brazil is a strong factor in the literature of the country, as well as in the politics. Nearly every politician is a writer, and, conversely, nearly every writer is more or less of a politician. Speeches are published in full, and politics and literature fill a large part of the space in the average Brazilian newspaper. The first newspaper established in Brazil was the *Gazeta do Rio*, in the year 1808, and other newspapers followed soon after in many other cities. The oldest paper in the capital, as well as the most influential one to-day, is the *Jornal do Comercio*, originally established as the *Spectator*, in 1824. Its contributors have included all the leading politicians and writers since that time. It is a large and well-printed newspaper of many pages, and is well edited. *O Paiz, Correio da Manhã, Jornal do Brazil, Gazeta de Noticias, Diario do Commercio, Diario de*

Noticias, *A Noticia*, *O Seculo*, *Correio da Noite* and *A Tribuna* are the other leading daily newspapers in the city to-day. *O Malho* and *Revista da Semana* are weekly reviews, while *O Tico-Tico* and *Fon-Fon* are illustrated comics. São Paulo, the second city, has a dozen daily newspapers, more than the average city of the United States of the same size. *O Estado de São Paulo* and the *Correio Paulistina* are the leading and most influential ones. The *Brazilian Review*, a weekly journal, is the only English periodical published in the country, but there are several German and Italian publications. There are also a number of class publications and trade journals, and nearly every town and city has a local daily or weekly publication.

The artistic sense is one of the essential elements of the Latin character. It has perhaps reached its highest development with the Italian race, but the Spaniards and the Portuguese also have this talent well developed. The traveller throughout Latin America can not fail to be impressed by the transplanted art that he finds everywhere in evidence. In Mexico, Central America and Peru he will find the original sense tinged with the Indian influence of the ancient races, who developed an architectural style of their own. Along the Atlantic coast of South America this element is lacking, because the Indians of that coast had not reached an advanced civilization, and lived in the crudest way. Hence the architecture of Brazil corresponds more nearly to the established schools that one will find in Latin Europe.

The Latin Americans strive for beauty, and, for myself, I must say that in general I admire their style. Some of their buildings would not appear well in a cold climate, but in design and decoration they are well adapted to the country. The government buildings, the plazas, the numerous statues, all have lines of beauty that please the eye. In small towns far from the railway one will oftentimes stumble upon a church, a convent or some other building of real artistic beauty and design. These buildings in a sense satisfy the artistic hunger of the race, and they are the objects to which every resident points with pride.

THE MUNICIPAL THEATRE, RIO DE JANEIRO.

The municipal theatre is one of these buildings that one will find in all the larger cities, where social life has attained anything of a metropolitan development, and even in smaller towns, where that stage has not been reached. It is constructed with the same care and regard for artistic proportions as the municipal building or the governmental palace, and, in many instances, with even more taste. The *teatro municipal*, as it is always named, is almost invariably built in an open place, where the view is unobstructed, while many of the public edifices are crowded up to the street line, and often hemmed in between surrounding buildings. Frequently it is exposed on all four sides, and an effort is made to give it an artistic appearance from whatever angle it is viewed, instead of limiting the artistic touches to the façade. Public money has been used for the construction of these buildings, and money from the same source, either municipal or national, is used to provide for the presentation of the drama or opera. It is only in this way that the best Italian, French, Portuguese and Spanish artists could ever be brought to Latin America, for the box receipts alone would not prove profitable. No one dreams of objecting to the use of the public money in this way, for the idea is inbred, and in accordance with the traditions of the race. This idea of practically subsidizing things artistic sounds strange to Anglo-Saxon ears, but among the Latins it is considered a proper function of government.

THE MUNICIPAL THEATRE, SÃO PAULO.

There are many beautiful opera houses in Brazil. At Manaos, a thousand miles up the Amazon, in a city surrounded on all sides by almost impenetrable forests, stands the Amazonas Theatre, a structure finished in white marble and richly decorated with allegorical paintings, the cost of which exceeded a million dollars in gold. In Pará, near the mouth of the same stream, is the La Paz Theatre, built by the state government, and which is a beautiful structure. Pernambuco, Bahia and many other cities have creditable theatres, but the *teatro municipal* of Rio de Janeiro, and the one at São Paulo, are the finest examples in Brazil, and perhaps in all of South America. The municipal theatre in São Paulo has not been entirely completed, although it has been in course of construction for several years. The interior and exterior are both richly decorated, the exterior with statues and allegorical designs, the interior with paintings. The musicians' stand is below the level of the orchestra seats in accordance with the Wagner system. The total cost will be about two million dollars in gold. The municipal theatre of Rio with its marble front, bronze decorations and beautiful dome one hundred and forty-seven and one-half feet high, which gives a crown effect, is the handsomest public building in that capital, and cost considerably more than the one at São Paulo. These municipal theatres are sometimes rented for other public functions, but in general the dignity and character of the entertainments is preserved.

CHAPTER XII
RAILWAYS AND THEIR DEVELOPMENT

Brazil has an excellent system of fluvial waterways throughout the Amazon district, where this great river and its many affluents give access to nearly every part of that basin. Upon these streams boats are run at regular or irregular intervals, which make connections with the regular lines on the Amazon running to Pará. The Amazon Steamship Company maintains forty small vessels on the Amazon and its tributaries, and there are other smaller companies operating in the same waters. Regular lines of steamers ply to the United States and Europe from Iquitos, Manaos and Pará. It will never be necessary, perhaps, to construct railroads through this richly watered country, except where rapids obstruct navigation, for railroad construction is difficult and the cost of transportation would necessarily be much more expensive. Coast lines run from Pará as far down as Rio de Janeiro, a journey of ten days to two weeks, including the various stops that are usually made. From Rio there are many lines that touch at Santos, and two Brazilian lines that run down as far as Rio Grande do Sul, the southernmost port. There is also communication by steamer from Rio up the Plata, Paraguay and Paraná Rivers to Cuyaba, capital of the state of Matto Grosso. In all there are several hundred vessels flying the Brazilian flag and operating either along the coast or on the rivers of the republic.

In the matter of railway communication there is very much to be desired still. There are in the entire republic to-day about twelve thousand miles of railway in operation. These lines are being extended at the rate of a few hundred miles each year. For the year 1909 the increase in mileage amounted to about six hundred miles. These extensions are being pushed out by a number of different lines into regions hitherto untouched by railway communication. These new lines have nearly all had a certain return, generally six per cent., guaranteed upon the capital invested by the federal or state governments. It speaks well for the condition of the country when one finds that many of these guarantees have never been called upon, for, almost from the very start, the traffic received has paid the running expenses, and even greater returns than those guaranteed to the company.

The great need of the country is a longitudinal railway, so that there will be continuous communication between Pará, at one extreme, and Rio Grande do Sul, at the other. In this respect better progress has been made in southern Brazil than in the northern part. It will not be many months, after this book is issued, until there will be an all rail route from Rio Grande do Sul to Rio de Janeiro, and from there for a considerable distance up into the state of Minas Geraes. This does not cover more than half of the distance, however, and it will be necessary to construct many hundreds of kilometres of the parallel iron rails before the project reaches completion. Pará, Camocim, Fortaleza, Pernambuco, Bahia, and other ports, have railroads which run inland for a greater or less distance, but are not connected up with the other systems. This makes it necessary for the passenger to take ship in going from one port to another, and for freight to be loaded upon steamers in order to reach the other than local markets of the country.

The local freight rates are so high, too, that it is often cheaper to ship freight from a European port to the capital, for instance, than to ship the same amount of freight from another part of the republic. This excessive charge for railway haul is a short-sighted policy, and does not tend to build up a local interchange between the different sections of the country. On the government railroad, the Central, the freight rates are so high between São Paulo and Rio de Janeiro, a distance of only three hundred miles, that it is cheaper to ship goods from the former city to Santos at high rates, transship them to a steamer, and pay port dues as well as loading and unloading charges at each end, than to forward over the railroad. It is a condition that the government could and should regulate, and it has been talked about many times; but, like many political projects, it has ended in talk. At the present time a commission has this matter in charge, and it remains to be seen what they will do.

What might be called the backbone of the railroad system of Brazil is the Estrado de Ferro Central do Brazil. This is one of the oldest lines in the country. There were about forty miles of it open to traffic as early as 1858. It was formerly known as the Dom Pedro II Railway, in honour of the Emperor, but upon the establishment of the republic the name was changed to the Central. The construction was first undertaken by an American company, but it was later taken over by the Imperial Government and completed by them to the city of São Paulo. The development and extension of the line has been almost continuous, until at the present time more than one thousand miles are in operation by this government railroad. The most of the track is of standard gauge, the same as the American lines, although a part of it is of the narrow gauge, one metre in width. The main line runs to São Paulo, and that is an important line, for it is the only railroad running to the important states of the south. The train service is good, and it pleases one to see American locomotives at the head of nearly all the trains, and many of the cars were built in American shops. The passenger coaches on all the Brazilian lines open at the end after the American plan, but the freight cars are built after the English models.

An important branch of this system is that which runs through Juiz de Fora, and to and beyond Bello Horizonte, in the State of Minas. This line passes through an important and well-settled section of the country, and is bringing the towns and rich valleys of that great state into direct communication with the capital. The upper part of this branch is narrow gauge, and it is being pushed northward to tap the rich mineral section of the state, where it is said that there are great quantities of manganese and other minerals awaiting development. Another branch is reaching out toward Diamantina, the famous diamond centre in Brazil. It seems to me that the government can not do better for itself, or for the people, than to spend just as much money as is possible in the development of these railway lines, for the land is already settled by a great many people, and easy communication will aid in inducing new settlers to locate there. Furthermore, railway communication is one of the best means in the world to unite the different sections of the country, and develop a national as well as patriotic spirit. The people of the states will feel that they have something in common, and interchange of traffic will also bring about a better acquaintance among the citizens of the various states. The operation of the Central Railroad has not been very successful from a financial standpoint, as too many sinecures have been created for political favourites. The cost of operation has always been excessive.

The Paulista Railway was the first railroad to be constructed entirely of Brazilian capital. Its tracks begin at Jundiahy, although its trains are run into the city of São Paulo. The proposition for this railroad was first offered to British capital, but they turned down what proved to be a veritable gold mine. The first work on this line was begun in 1870, and its tracks have been gradually extended until now it operates about seven hundred miles of road, about one-third of which is standard and the balance metre gauge. It reaches to Bebedouroa and Pontat, with branches to Jahu and other points. By the original contract the government guaranteed seven per cent. on the investment required, but this guarantee was later released by the company in return for some other favours. It has the right to raise tariffs in order to keep the investment on a seven per cent. basis, but the present high freight rates yield returns far in excess of that. One part of the concession of this road is a privileged zone of nearly twenty miles on each side, within which district it has the exclusive right of both passenger and freight traffic. It reaches up into the *terra roxa*, the red earth where the blood-red soil dyes everything its own colour. This is the coffee land, the great freight producer for this line. In one year, 1906, this line carried nearly ten million bags of coffee, each bag weighing about one hundred and thirty-two pounds, besides all the other miscellaneous freight.

The Mogyana Railway is another narrow gauge railroad which starts at Campinas, and runs in a northerly direction up through the coffee country. It was started shortly after the Paulista Railway, and upon practically the same guaranty of the investment, and the same rights to exclusive territory. Branches have been built for feeders, and the main line has been extended, until now this company has a mileage of more than eight hundred miles. The road was evidently built by the kilometre, and the contractors got in as many kilometres between given points as possible. Beautiful curves abound everywhere, and it would be difficult to find a straight half-mile of track between Campinas and Riberão Preto, a distance of about two hundred miles. The line is well built and is now being ballasted. A few sections have been straightened out, but it contains dozens of unnecessary and nerve-racking curves. This railway is also a great freight producer, especially for coffee. It has paid dividends of twelve per cent. for several years, and could probably have paid more except for charter restrictions. The furthermost point now reached by this railroad is Araguary, in the state of Minas Geraes. From Araguary this company has in contemplation the extension of its line to Goyaz, in the state of Goyaz. For the good of the country it is to be hoped that this project will be carried out in the near future.

Goyaz is as large as France, Belgium, Holland and England combined, is very similar in topography to Minas Geraes, and also contains considerable mineral wealth. Politically it is in the centre of the republic. The maps show a great square block in this state which is marked "site for the future capital of Brazil." It will be many years, however, before this project will be realized, and not until railroads are constructed, for at the present time there is not a mile of railroad track in the state. The site is a delightful one among the mountains. There are splendid natural resources in Goyaz, but the population scarcely exceeds one to the square mile. The river Maranhão traverses the state, almost from one end to the other, and it is navigable by small vessels for hundreds of miles within the state. The Araguaya marks the western boundary, and is also navigable for a long distance. Both of these rivers are affluents of the Tocantins, which pours its waters into the Amazon flood.

The Sorocabana Railway system is an important line in this section of the state and promises much for its future development, as it is pushing extensions in several directions. It is now operated by an American corporation made up of Canadian, American and English capitalists. The main line begins at São Paulo, and then branches out in several different directions, northwest, west and southwest, and will eventually be the connecting link between the trunk lines to the western and southern states. It is thus destined to be one of the greatest railroad systems in the republic. The Sorocabana is also a narrow gauge railway. It has a government guarantee of six and seven per cent., and a privileged zone on each side gives it a local monopoly. This company took the lines over from the state government of São Paulo, and they have obtained a number of valuable privileges.

The Sorocabana Railway Company now operates about seven hundred miles of railroad. One branch has its terminus at Jundiahy, and from there runs through the important city of Piracicaba. From Jundiahy to Piracicaba it passes through a great deal of undeveloped country, but at the latter place it reaches one of the prettiest sections I have seen in Brazil. As far as the eye can reach the eye falls upon cultivated fields of coffee, sugar cane, corn, fruit, etc. In the distance the horizon is everywhere bounded by the hills, which seem to form a frame for the picture. The city itself is clean and attractive, with wide streets, and beautiful plazas. It is situated on a knoll with all the streets slightly sloping down, so that in the distance one can see the green fields and boundary of mountains. It has a good sugar factory, owned by a French syndicate, a cotton mill and other industries. The finest sight is the falls on the Piracicaba River, which are within the city itself. These falls are beautiful and furnish thousands of horse power, only a portion of which is now utilized.

The main line extends from São Paulo to Bauru, a distance of three hundred miles, and passes through some rich coffee lands which are now being developed.

At Bauru the Sorocabana connects with the Nord Oeste do Brazil (Northwestern), which is a projected line to run across the immense state of Matto Grosso and into Bolivia. The projectors believe that this line will eventually be a part of the proposed Pan American railroad. Construction has been completed up to Itapura, on the Tieté River near its junction with the Alta Paraná, and trains are now running to that village. The most of the line after Bauru follows the general course of the Tieté River, and passes through an entirely undeveloped country, much of which is forest land where large quantities of fine hardwood timber are found. This is the first railroad to touch the borders of the great undeveloped state of Matto Grosso, and it means much for that state. At Miranda, a hundred miles or more of grade has been completed, and work is being pushed from that town toward Itapura. Materials and supplies are sent up through the Rio de la Plata and its connections. Many hundreds of miles of this projected trunk line have not yet been touched, although preliminary surveys have been made over the entire distance.

To the southwest the Sorocabana Railway passes through rich coffee and cotton lands to Itarare. Here it connects with the São Paulo-Rio Grande Railway, which is also one of the important links in the lines connecting up the Southern states, Uruguay and Argentina. From Itarare the São Paulo-Rio Grande Railway runs in a southerly direction through Ponta Grossa, to the banks of the Uruguay River, where it will connect with the Santa Maria and Uruguay Railway. It already has in operation over four hundred miles. Only a couple of hundred miles are uncompleted to make a continuous line, with the various connections, from Rio de Janeiro to Rio Grande do Sul, and Montevideo, Uruguay. The charter of this company also involves the building of a railroad from the port of São Francisco at right angles to and crossing the main line, following the Iguassú River to where it empties into the Alta Paraná. The concession of this line gives it all the unoccupied lands on either side for six miles, with the obligation to settle the same within fifty years. This was done by the government to induce the railroad company to encourage immigration, and populate the country. The company also agrees to settle one block of land with immigrants for each one hundred kilometres of track, each block to contain one hundred lots suitable for agriculture or cattle raising, within two years after the approval of each completed section.

The Santa Maria and Uruguay Railway runs at present from near Passo Fundo, south through Cruz Alta to Santa Maria, where it connects with the line which crosses the state of Rio Grande do Sul, from the prosperous port of Porto Alegre to Uruguayana, on the Uruguay River, the boundary line with Argentina, and there connects with the lines of that republic. This railroad passes through a rich country, and along its line many colonies have been established which have become very prosperous. The climate of this state is cooler, and resembles that of large sections of the United States. At Cacequy there is a branch to the city of Bagé, where numerous *xarqueados* are established, and from there runs to Pelotas and the city of Rio Grande. From near Bagé, also, a branch is being extended toward the borders of Uruguay, and probably before this book appears there will be continuous communication by this route with Montevideo, the capital of that republic.

From Montevideo it is but a few hours ride by comfortable steamer to Buenos Aires, where connection is made with the extensive railway systems of that republic. By way of the Buenos Aires al Pacifico and Transandine lines through rail communication now exists to Valparaiso and Santiago, Chile, and the rich "Valley of Paradise," south of the latter city. In a year or two also it will be possible to go by rail from Buenos Aires, via the Central Argentina and the government lines, up to La Paz, the capital of Bolivia. The Peruvian government has also a project for a railroad across the Andes from Lima to La Paz, although this is far from being realized as yet. It simply gives an idea of the railway development that has taken place, and what is projected for the future.

North of Rio de Janeiro there has not been so much or so systematic railway development, as there has been south of the federal capital. The principal company operating in that direction, the Leopoldina Railway, is also the company having the greatest mileage of any road in the republic.

Its lines traverse the states of Rio de Janeiro, Espirito Santo and Minas Geraes, and have a total mileage of over eighteen hundred miles. This system has been made up by the consolidation of a number of different lines. Hitherto it has not been able to run its track into the city of Rio de Janeiro, because of the opposition of the Central, which road claimed a monopoly. Its terminals have been at Nictheroy across the bay, and at Mauá. At last the right was granted, a depot constructed, and, by this time, the trains of the Leopoldina Railway will be running into the capital city. They promise service from that city to Petropolis in a little over an hour, instead of two hours by the present combination of rail and boat. This line taps rich coffee and sugar lands, reaches back into the mineral section of Minas Geraes, and passes near lands where fine timbers, such as rosewood, abound. It also connects with the port of Victoria, which is destined to be an important port for the products of this district. One of the lines is gradually being pushed up toward Bahia, and will eventually connect with the lines of that state, of which there are three or four spurs that spread inland in different directions from the city of Bahia.

The state of Espirito Santo (Holy Spirit) tapped by the Leopoldina system, stretches along the Atlantic coast for nearly three hundred miles. With an area of twenty thousand square miles it has a population of less than twelve to the square mile. It is a tropical state with much rain and dense vegetation along the coast lowlands. The capital city, Victoria, has a good harbour which is now being improved by the national government. In coffee shipments this port ranks third in importance. A railroad is also being constructed from Victoria to Diamantina, but progress up to date has been rather slow.

The next largest system in northern Brazil is the Great Western Railway, whose lines run from Maceio, in the state of Alagoas, through Recife, or Pernambuco, capital of the state of that name, Parahyba, capital of the state of Parahyba, and ending at Natal, capital and chief seaport of the state of Rio Grande do Norte. A number of branches wind their tortuous way inland, and each year extensions are being made. The total length of the lines of this company now exceed nine hundred miles, upon all of which a government guarantee of at least six per cent. exists. These lines were formerly operated under several different names, but have recently been consolidated.

In the state of Ceará there are two railways. One connects the port and capital city, Fortaleza, with Senador Pompeu, a couple of hundred miles inland; another line runs from the port of Camocim to the interior town of Ipu. A short railway connects Caxias, on the river Itapucurú, with Floris, on the Paranahyba River. This is the only railway in the state of Maranhão, the sixth state in the republic and as large as Texas. Its natural resources have hardly been investigated, but they are no doubt very rich. St. Luiz is the capital and one of the ports. The adjoining state of Piauhy has no railroad. There is, however, excellent river communication with the seaports. A railway is projected from the port of Santo Luiz to run down and connect with the line now running from Bahia north. From Belem, or Pará, there is one short railroad that runs to Braganca, a distance of about one hundred miles.

The Madeira-Mamoré railroad is an isolated railroad, being built in the western part of Brazil by an American company under contract with the Brazilian government. One must go a thousand miles up the Amazon, and then six hundred and sixty miles up the Madeira River to Santo Antonio de Rio Madeira, where this line begins, and which is in the very heart of South America. Above the rapids there are several hundred more miles of navigable waters, upon which a service of steamers is maintained. There are few people in that section of the country, and it may never be popular with immigrants. The line is being constructed in pursuance of an agreement with the Republic of Bolivia when the Acre (pronounced Ack'ray) territory was ceded by that government to Brazil. The rich eastern slope and fertile plains of Bolivia are practically bottled up. Its products, including a large rubber and cacao production, either had to be transported over the Andes, or around a couple of hundred miles of rapids and cataracts on the Madeira River, to the part of the stream where navigation is uninterrupted. From there they were carried down on steamers to Manaos, or Pará, and then to the markets of the world by ocean-going vessels. This line will be about two hundred miles in length, and will open up one of the richest sections of Bolivia, a part of Peru, which also borders on the Acre territory, and the rich territory itself, which produces a large amount of rubber and cacao, and much of which has never been exploited at all. Many native Indians inhabit this section, and their little rafts and row boats navigate all the streams. In these the Indian rubber gatherers visit the different sections, tap the trees, and bring the rubber to the establishments of the various companies engaged in the rubber trade, which may be found in many places.

The first sod for this railway was turned in 1871, but this auspicious beginning soon ended in disaster. Again, in 1878, a second attempt was made, and work was prosecuted faithfully for a year. A survey was cut through the almost impenetrable forest, and four miles of track were completed. At that time, however, sanitation was not understood as well as now, and the great mortality stopped the work, as it did in Panama. This time a sensible beginning was made by first looking after the health conditions, and practically the same methods are employed as are followed by the United States on the Isthmus. Sanitary buildings were erected with provision made against infection from mosquito bites, and a fully equipped hospital was built and furnished. By these means the health of the twenty-five hundred employees has been looked after in a thoroughly scientific way. At the present writing about fifty miles of track have been completed, and a dozen engines are already at work. Forces of workmen are engaged in cutting down the forest, grading, laying track and rails, and all the other processes incidental to building a railroad. Nature has not changed one iota, for malarial fever is still malarial fever, the rainfall is as great as ever, and vegetation is just as luxuriant; but science has taught man how to conquer nature, and it will not be many years until locomotives will be hauling freight and passengers around these falls in a few hours, where formerly it required weeks. Americans may take a pardonable interest in this project, for it is American energy and American equipment that is doing the work.

THE SÃO PAULO RAILWAY, NEAR SANTOS.

I have reserved for the last one of the most important, as well as one of the most interesting railroads in the world, the São Paulo Railway. This line is important, not from the amount of mileage, for it only runs from the port of Santos to Jundiahy, a distance of about one hundred miles, but because of the amount of freight shipped over it. It is the only railroad in the state of São Paulo running to the coast, and all the products of that state are shipped over it. Two-thirds or more of the world's coffee is produced in Brazil, and of this three-fourths is shipped from this one port, and all of it hauled over this one road. As high as thirteen million sacks of coffee, weighing sixty kilograms each, have been shipped from this port in a single year. It has a monopoly of thirty-one kilometers on each side of the track. This restriction heretofore has prevented any other railroad from entering Santos, although both the Mogyana and the Sorocobana have surveyed routes and projected lines to it, because of the excessive freight rates charged. Both of the other roads are narrow gauge, and the expense of reloading for a short journey, and the rates demanded by this monopolistic line, are a big drain on the revenues of the other railroads.

The São Paulo Railway originally held a seven per cent. guarantee from the government, but this was long ago released. Its earnings have been so great in some years that the company did not know what to do with the surplus. It was allowed to pay only twelve per cent. to the stockholders, and the balance must either be paid to the state or the rates reduced. Unwilling to do either, this company has built fine stations where there are not more than a score of people, and has expended money in every way to keep down the net earnings under that sum. For six miles, soon after leaving Santos, the road climbs the Serra do Mar by means of cables. This is divided into four sections, each with its own power station. The trains are run in sections of three or four cars each, with an engine on each section. One section goes up as another comes down on each cable. A few years ago the traffic became so congested that it was necessary to construct a second roadway over the Serra, the one roadbed being considerably lower than the other. The mountainside is paved in some places to prevent landslides. Water courses and gullys of masonry and cement have been constructed everywhere to carry away the rain, which sometimes falls here with almost the force of a cloudburst. The road is well ballasted with a crushed stone found in the hills which is as hard as granite. The Luz station in the city of São Paulo, belonging to this company, is by far the finest station in South America, and one of the finest in the world. The railroad is owned by an English company, and the engines and equipment are distinctly English, and the entire track is built with the care and precision of an English railroad, with an overhead bridge or tunnel at each station to pass from the station on one side of the track to that on the other. The road has only one little branch in addition to the main line.

CHAPTER XIII
COFFEE

Brazil is not only the land where the nuts come from, but it is also the land where the world's coffee comes from as well. Two-thirds, and possibly three-fourths, of all the coffee used in the world is produced by this one great country. It matters little whether your grocer labels your coffee Mocha, Java, or any other name, it is a pretty safe guess to say that it was raised in Brazil. Richer than gold have proven the stretches of red soil where this berry grows. This soil occurs at intervals from the state of Pernambuco south almost to Rio Grande do Sul, the southernmost state. Of Brazil's production three-fourths or more is grown in the state of São Paulo, thus making the production of this one state alone more than half of the world's production. Considering the enormous quantity of coffee consumed, this product and its cultivation in Brazil becomes of world-wide interest.

The name coffee is derived from Kaffa, a town in Arabia, where it was first grown. Coffee began to be introduced into Europe in the fifteenth century, where coffee houses were established and soon became very popular. In Turkey and England they later came under royal displeasure; in the former country, because the seduction of the beverage kept the people from the services of the mosque, and caused them to ignore the hours for prayer; in the latter, because the coffee houses were believed to be places of sedition, and disloyalty to the crown. In spite of royal displeasure and the restrictions of the government, however, the use of the coffee beverage continually grew, and the restrictive measures seemed to have little effect on its use.

About the middle of the eighteenth century the cultivation was introduced into the New World, in Guatemala, Mexico, the West Indies and Brazil. In the latter country it is said to have been introduced about 1761, by a deserter who came to that country and brought with him a few seeds. Its cultivation was, however, on a very small scale for a number of decades, but was gradually introduced into a number of states where it was found adapted to the soil. It was not until early in the nineteenth century that the cultivation of this plant on a large scale was begun at Campinas, and within a few years the production had reached an important figure. In the first year of that century it is said that two bags were sent to foreign markets from Brazil. A dozen years later the shipment of bags was numbered by the thousands, until, in 1817, the exports are reported to have been in excess of sixty thousand bags. The state of São Paulo from the very first took the lead in production of coffee, as the soil of that state seemed especially adapted to its cultivation. In this state alone, at the present time, it is estimated that there are nearly seven hundred millions of trees, and the annual production will average more than ten million sacks, or one billion three hundred and twenty million pounds of this berry. These figures will not be materially altered for several years, because of the restrictive legislation prohibiting the planting of new trees, which will be explained more in detail later.

Successful cultivation of coffee, like that of almost any other valuable crop, requires certain conditions of soil and climate. These are a rich earth, a certain rarefication of air and plenty of moisture. The *terra roxa* (red earth) of Brazil is very rich, and is the result of the decomposition of rocks of basaltic origin. The best lands are at an altitude of one thousand five hundred feet, or more, above sea level and require eighty inches or more of annual rainfall. Furthermore, hilly lands with an eastern exposure are generally chosen. Although plantations are sometimes found on comparatively level ground. Too much or too little moisture, or a frost, will spoil a season's crop. A coffee field, with its trees laid out in regular rows stretching as far as the eye can see to the top of the hills in either direction, is a beautiful sight. In the foreground the rows of trees, with the roads at regular intervals and the contrast of green against the red soil, are plainly visible; but, as distance increases, they blend together until the whole seems a field of living green, gently swaying in the breeze. Like a great panorama these fields spread out in every direction in the neighbourhood of Riberão Preto, the centre of the richest coffee district.

Coffee trees are a matter of slow growth, requiring at least four years to mature after the young plants are set out. The seed is always planted in the woods, where patches are cleared for that purpose, and where the necessary shade and moisture are found. They are always transplanted during the rainy season, when about eighteen months old and perhaps a foot high, and during this work the tender plants are handled very carefully. In many countries the young trees are shaded by banana stalks, but that method is not followed in Brazil. Corn is oftentimes planted between the rows of coffee trees to bring an extra crop, but this method is not approved by the best planters, as coffee trees exhaust the soil rapidly enough by themselves. On some of the old *fazendas* the plants are set in rows not more than eight or ten feet apart, but the newer plantations are at a distance of from twelve to fifteen feet. The trees are carefully pruned, and the ground weeded each year, and a crop will be produced about the fifth year after planting. If the trees are left to grow untrimmed they will reach a height of eighteen or twenty feet, but they are usually kept down to a height of about twelve feet, or less, and are not allowed to spread out too much. One quickly learns to distinguish between a well-kept and a poorly-cultivated coffee plantation by its trimmed or untrimmed appearance. The growth of weeds is sometimes allowed, especially on hillsides, as the roots of the weeds prevent the soil from washing during the tropical downpours. Otherwise the rich surface dirt will disappear down into the valleys below. A planter's credit was at one time determined by the number of trees he owned, and that was the reason that some of the fields were planted so closely together. It has been proven, however, by experience, that close planting does not pay. One of the most successful planters told me that even the wagon roads, which are left at intervals of perhaps five hundred feet, were not a loss, for the trees on each side produced so much more abundantly that they made up for the row or two of trees left out for the road.

The coffee tree is an evergreen, and usually has a single trunk with many branches. The leaves are long, smooth and dark green in appearance. They are almost a shiny green like the holly, and look as though they had been varnished. The blossoms grow in great abundance in the axils of the branches, and a field in blossom is most entrancing. In the early morning, after a refreshing shower, or while the dew still lingers, the fields with their small, white blossoms are not only a beautiful sight to the eye, but an aroma arises from them that fills the air with a sweet perfume. The fruit usually grows in clusters of from a half dozen to a dozen berries, which surround the joints almost like a necklace just over the leaves. When ripe, the coffee berries resemble very much a cranberry of medium size. Then the coffee field is again a pretty picture, for the white flowers have turned into beautiful red berries, and the bushes resemble richly loaded cherry trees. The tree will produce abundant crops after the sixth year, and I saw fields that were at least thirty-five years old, and still bearing profitable crops. It is said that the coffee trees will produce as long as the life of man. There are two kinds of trees cultivated in Brazil: the common and the yellow-berried, or Botucatu, and generally called the Bourbon. The yellow-berried variety develops more rapidly, and gives more abundant crops, but its cultivation is more difficult. This latter is the one most generally cultivated at the present time, but it brings a lower price because it is said to be inferior to the other in aromatic qualities and the weight of the grain. Its introduction came about when the price was very high and every planter was anxious to obtain as great a production as possible.

The coffee trees begin to blossom in September and continue to bloom for several weeks. The maturing process is also irregular, and covers a period of a couple of months. It requires a number of months for the berries to mature, and in the state of São Paulo, for instance, the first picking does not take place until the last of May or first of June. From that time on the plantations are scenes of activity for five or six months, until the last of the crop is dispatched to the commission houses in Santos. The fields will then be filled with men, women and children with their baskets, gathering up the precious fruit, ready to be taken to the drying yards.

At harvesting time thousands of pickers flock to the coffee regions from other parts of Brazil, as they are able to earn good wages for a few weeks. Many whole families will travel for days on foot, when they have not enough money to pay their railroad fares. There is often considerable rivalry among the pickers to see who can pick the most; but there is also the further incentive to rapid work in the fact that all wages are paid at so much for a fixed quantity. Fifty pounds is considered a good day's picking when it is done from the trees. The method in general operation on the large *fazendas* is to strip the branches of all their coffee berries, by pulling them between the fingers, and then others follow up and pick up the berries, leaves, etc., from the ground, or the sheets which have been spread out to catch them. In this way only one picking is made even though some of the berries have become overripe, and others are green owing to the uneven ripening. This causes a considerable unavoidable loss. In an extraordinary season a tree may produce as much as seven pounds of coffee, but a fair average is three pounds per tree.

DRYING COFFEE.

The gathering and preparation of the berries is a difficult and laborious operation involving a number of processes. The large plantations are equipped with all the necessary paved yards and machinery for this work, and the smaller planters send theirs to central factories, or *beneficios*, as they are called. The coffee must be washed, pulped, dried and submitted to several stages of preparation. The washing is a simple process, but the work of drying requires the greatest care, for it exercises a great influence on the value of the coffee. There are at least two distinct processes in the preparation of the coffee, but it is always first washed and then soaked in order to soften the pulp, so that it can be removed, for the coffee beans are in the centre. This "pulping" is done by a revolving cylinder set with teeth, after which the beans are run into tanks for a thorough washing to remove all traces of the pulp.

Some have a series of these tanks through which the coffee is passed, and the beans are then carried by means of running water out through the paving yards. On these great yards of beaten earth, paved with bricks or cemented, and sometimes tarred (for they dry quicker on a tarred floor), the berries are spread out in thin layers to dry. If you would take up a handful at this time you would find they were covered with a soft gummy substance. No artificial drying process equals that of the sun's rays. Men with wooden rakes, and in their bare feet, are kept constantly busy turning over the berries to hasten this process, which oftentimes requires many days, and even weeks, for it is necessary that they be evenly dried.

You probably expect to see a green berry or bean at this time but they are still covered with a parchment-like skin. When they are finally dried this parchment skin is removed by passing the beans through heavy rollers, and the chaff is cleared away by machine work similar to that used for similar processes in wheat threshing and cleaning. By a continuous process the beans are passed through machines which husk, fan, polish and sort them according to sizes. The berries are now a light olive-green colour. The little round beans are classed as "Mocha" and another size as "Java," etc. The various grades are then sacked in coarse sacks, labelled with the name of the *fazenda* and the grade, and shipped to Rio de Janeiro, or Santos, where the great commission houses are located.

The commission houses are important institutions and practically own many of the *fazendas* through advance loans, and the planter is helpless against charges that are oftentimes excessive. In the warehouses the coffee is all emptied out in great piles, and repacked in new sacks, often being regraded by the commissionaires. The planter is burdened with a great number of expenses. The net price to him the past year was only a little over four cents per pound. Among these expenses the following is a fair list as taken from an official publication, and verified to me by a leading planter: transportation to the railroad station, transportation to Santos, municipal export tax, resacking charges, shipping old sacks back, brokers' commission (should be three per cent., but is in fact much higher), a special tax of $1.00 per sack and an *ad valorem* export tax of nine per cent., and a number of other minor charges. In the end it is the commission man who has the smallest amount of work and least risk, who makes the big money at the present price of coffee. It used to be when the planter received ten to twelve cents per pound for his coffee that the *fazendero* rolled in wealth, and no extravagance or luxury was beyond him. At the present time only those who have the latest improved machinery, so that the cost of preparation is reduced to a minimum, are making much money. A rise or fall of a cent per pound often means prosperity to the coffee producer or the reverse. The price to-day is not more than one-third of what it was a number of years ago. It is probably quite possible to simplify the cultivation of coffee trees so that there would be a considerable margin of profit at the present prices. One progressive planter looks after forty thousand trees with one man, four mules and two machines of a recent pattern, according to a report that I saw.

The steady decrease in the price of coffee during several years led to a new departure in economics, by the three great coffee producing states of Brazil. A sack of coffee (one hundred and thirty-two pounds), which in 1895 was worth almost $20.00 in Europe, had fallen to $8.00 in 1905. The coffee planters were almost in despair over this low price, which threatened to spell ruin for many of them within a short time. Among themselves they had attempted various measures, but all of them had failed. An attempt had been made as early as 1901, by the state of São Paulo, to remedy this situation, by a practically prohibitive tax upon new plantations, allowing each planter to set out each year only five per cent. of what he already possessed. This would not much more than replace the natural decay. This order was originally made for a period of five years, but has since been continued for another period of the same length.

This measure failed to bring about the desired result. Finally, when the crop of 1906-7 promised to be such an unusual crop, the planters appealed to the government for further relief. The state was equally interested, since by far the greatest part of the revenue of the state, and the various municipalities as well, is derived from its tax upon coffee, and they were afraid that the planters would become panicky and abandon coffee cultivation. Because of this alarm the governments of the three states of Rio de Janeiro, Minas Geraes and São Paulo entered into an agreement, known as the Taubaté Agreement, by which these states, acting through São Paulo, agreed to buy up on the market the surplus production and store it until such time as, in the judgment of the commissioners, conditions warranted its sale.

This judgment was based upon the observation that coffee trees exhaust themselves by such an extraordinary crop, and yield only average crops for the next two or three years. They figured that by that time the natural increase in the consumption would give a market for this coffee. Further, it was known that coffee improves, rather than deteriorates, with age. A special export tax of $0.60 to $1.00 per sack was established at the ports of Rio and Santos, and the government of São Paulo was authorized to borrow not to exceed $45,000,000 to raise a fund to purchase the coffee, each of the three states jointly binding themselves in the obligation. As a result of this agreement that state purchased eight million sacks of coffee in the market, and these were stored in a number of central points in Europe, as well as in New York. Money was borrowed at comparatively high rates. Both the state obligation was given and the stored coffee pledged as collateral security. At that time it was estimated that there would be, including the new crop, a surplus stock of fourteen million sacks of coffee, representing almost one year's consumption.

The result of this action of the coffee producing states has not been what was expected. The price has not increased as was predicted, and the interest and other expenses have been a great drain upon revenues. Another part of the scheme was to limit the exportations from the country; nine million sacks being fixed for the year 1908, nine million five hundred thousand for the year 1909, and ten million for the following years. All coffee exported above that amount would be subject to an additional tax which made it prohibitive. Furthermore, the crops were rather larger than was expected, so that the surplus stock had not appreciatively decreased. In the winter of 1909-10, the time of my visit, there was a movement on foot, which gained a great many adherents, to arbitrarily destroy ten per cent. of the previous season's crop, but this was not done. Within four months after the new crop came in, the limit allowed for export had been reached, and the export trade was at a standstill. It was a new attempt to get around the law of supply and demand. The final result of this attempt is as yet problematical, and remains to be seen. It was a bold and original effort that has many defenders, and many critics as well, right among the Brazilian people.

If not the best, the Brazilians make one of the best cups of coffee in the world. Never have I tasted such delicious coffee as I did almost all over that republic. The Brazilians understand fully the art of preparing this delicious beverage, and make it fit for kings and queens. They generally choose a coffee berry at least two years old, as they say that age improves the aroma. Some even say that five or six years' storage in a dry place is still better. Another essential, they say, is to roast and grind the coffee fresh every day. The roasting process is very thorough, for it is roasted until the average

American housewife would call it burned. The black roasted coffee is reduced to a fine powder, and then placed in a woollen bag through which hot water is poured. It is *never* allowed to boil, so that their coffee is rather a percolation than an extraction. I am not a cook, but I do know that the coffee as prepared by the Brazilians is delicious, and seems to be free from the harmful effects. In the morning it is served in about equal proportions with hot milk, but at all other times clear. Little dainty cups of black coffee with plenty of damp sugar are always served at social calls, at nearly all public offices and in many other places where one visits. In fact, if you called on a Brazilian family, and coffee or some other refreshment were not served, you would almost be justified in believing that your call was not especially welcome. I drank coffee many times, and at all hours, when offered, and often feared the consequences, but never felt the slightest ill effect.

CHAPTER XIV
THE LAND AND SEA FORCES

"You had better take off your hat," said a friend to me, as some national troops were marching by on the Avenida Central, in Rio de Janeiro; "if you do not, some one may knock it off," he continued. Then I noticed that every man and boy respectfully lifted his hat as the flag passed him; and I did the same. Three regiments of infantry passed along, each with its banner fluttering in the breeze, and as many times did we lift our hats in salute to the green and yellow starred emblem of Brazil; and I must confess that the sentiment involved in this tribute to the flag, for which we are supposed to be willing to bleed and die at all times, is commendable, and worthy of emulation.

Brazil is not a military nation in the sense that European nations are such. The proportion of soldiers to the population is greater than in the United States, but far less than in almost any European nation. The total number of men under arms, including the military police, does not exceed fifty thousand men. Of this number more than one-half are state troops. The soldiers are not much in evidence in any part of the republic, except those doing police duty. A compulsory military service does not exist, after the German or French model, although the right of conscription by either state or federal government is a part of the law, and can be resorted to whenever, in the judgment of either government, such a step becomes necessary. Retired or active officers are stationed at nearly all the colleges, by whom instruction in military tactics is given after established systems, much the same as in our own educational institutions. The term of enlistment in the federal army is for three years, with certain privileges in the event that the soldier re-enlists when a term has expired. One of these privileges is the choice of a free grant of land in one of the government colonies, and the gift of an outfit of agricultural implements with which to cultivate it.

Another inducement is in the way of additional remuneration. The entire republic is divided into seven districts, in each of which a barrack is maintained. The federal troops are divided into twenty different regiments, and a number of battalions are made up of the different branches of the service. The arms of all troops are of the latest improved Mauser type, and the artillery is exclusively of German manufacture.

The state troops number a considerable force. They are different in organization from the state militia of the United States, because they are regular troops under arms. The most of them serve in the various cities of the states as military police. They are a good and effective force in preserving order; and yet they have often been the source of serious trouble, for this system has enabled a state ring to defy national authority, because they had right at hand an armed force of their own, which primarily owned allegiance to the state government. The state of São Paulo alone has in its employ a force that exceeds five thousand well-armed and trained troops. Rio Grande do Sul, that turbulent and impetuous southern state, has an almost equal force, and the "Rio Grandenses" have been proven puissant and effective in more than one skirmish with federal troops. Bahia maintains about three thousand soldiers under arms in her barracks, and Minas Geraes comes next with twenty-five hundred. There is not a single state which does not have at least a few hundred men enrolled under its own banner. If all of these state troops would be loyal to the federal government, as they undoubtedly would be at this time, it would give a fairly good fighting force with which to meet any aggression from without.

The revolt of a national navy seems like a very unusual and almost ludicrous proceeding; yet Brazil had such an experience early in the history of the republic. For six months the Brazilian navy under Admirals Mello and Saldanha da Gama openly defied the authority of President Floriano, the second incumbent of that high office. Admiral Mello, who was in command of the navy, sent a short and curt message to the President ordering him to resign the presidency within six hours, or a bombardment of Rio de Janeiro would follow. President Floriano was made of stern stuff and flatly refused to resign. The Admiral then weakened in his threat and did not bombard the capital. Had he carried it out great destruction would undoubtedly have followed. The most of the navy remained in the bay, but a few of the boats escaped and joined the land insurgents in the southern part of the republic. The navy, cut off from supplies of food and fuel, was obliged to yield in the end, and the national government was victorious.

A quarter of a century ago the Brazilian navy was easily the most powerful in the southern hemisphere. At that time no other South American republic could boast of a navy of any considerable strength. Brazil then possessed a number of battleships, cruisers and other boats that were very creditable, and the cost of which had been very great. Since that time both Argentina and Chile have spent large sums of money building up their naval strength, and the discrepancy in sea forces is not so great as formerly. Both of these nations have made great financial sacrifices in order to dispute the supremacy of their bulky neighbour on the water. Ever since the establishment of an independent empire in Brazil more attention had been devoted to building up a formidable sea force than an army, and the same conditions exist to-day. It is perhaps not a bad thing for Brazil to have a strong navy because of its extensive coast line. Furthermore, because of the loose cohesion between the states, this arm of the national government adds greatly to its prestige. Nearly all the most powerful states have an extensive sea coast, and the navy would greatly assist the federal government in the event of any revolt against its authority. Although each state has its own military force, as heretofore described, none of them have any armed vessels to protect their ports. It is quite possible also, that a united interest in a powerful navy may aid in furthering a national and federal spirit which will aid in breaking down the idea of state loyalty as against federal unity, which has been hitherto predominant. If this should be the result, then the money invested in these seemingly useless monsters of the deep may be well spent.

The only instance when the navy has been in actual service was during the conflict with Argentina, and the Paraguayan war, when some engagements took place on the Paraná and Paraguay Rivers, between some of the smaller boats of Brazil and some armed vessels of Paraguay. In these encounters the former were victorious, and the Brazilians are proud of referring to the glorious traditions of the history of their navy.

The principal naval establishment is at Rio de Janeiro, near the landing dock. The naval yards here are quite extensive, and a couple of thousand men are usually employed. Several small cruisers and some river boats have been constructed there, but all the large boats have been built abroad, and the most of them in British yards. At the present time the boats listed in the Brazilian navy number about fifty. This includes every vessel, large and small, many of which are practically useless from the modern view point of practical war values. They could only be used in patrolling inland rivers, where neither armed vessels nor forts would be encountered. This list includes seven vessels that are classed as battleships, eight cruisers, nine torpedo boats, and then the auxiliary fleet, consisting of several small gun boats, dispatch boats, etc.

This list does not embody, however, the new vessels which are now being received from English builders. A couple of years ago contracts were let for three Dreadnaughts, two scout ships, two torpedo boats and ten torpedo boat destroyers. The addition of these boats will again place Brazil in the first rank of naval powers in the southern hemisphere. The three Dreadnaughts are claimed by the Brazilians to be the most powerful of their kind that have yet been constructed. They contain some new modifications in the placing of armour and the equipment of guns.

These monster warships will be named the Minas Geraes, São Paulo and the Rio de Janeiro, in honour of the three most powerful states. The first named has already been delivered, and is now in Brazilian waters. The other two will follow at intervals of a few months, and the smaller boats will all be added to the navy during the year 1910. One innovation is the placing of twelve-inch guns in the upper towers instead of the ten-inch guns which have been used heretofore. This feature, the British builders claim, gives these boats the most powerful armament of any ships afloat. Nine-inch armour has been used where seven and eight inch has generally been used. Then secondary batteries of great strength have been added in the centre line of the boats, which are also a novel feature. A speed of almost twenty-two knots an hour for these leviathans has been generated by the builders on the several trial runs. Each of the new battleships will be five hundred and forty-three feet in length with a displacement of nineteen thousand two hundred and eighty tons and a draught of twenty-five feet. The two scout ships will be named Bahia and Rio Grande do Sul after two more states. These vessels have been built for speed, and will be able to rush through the water at the rate of twenty-six and one-half knots per hour. They are now considering the advisability of adding submarine boats to the navy in order to complete the naval equipment.

"These new ships," say the Brazilian authorities, "make it impossible for the great powers to start any so-called pacific demonstration against Brazil.

To have any chance of success against the Brazilian Dreadnaughts, and other subsidiary ships, a power ought to have a number of ships at least double; but there is no country, England included, that can send so far from home such a considerable part of its navy without danger." It has had one effect, and that has been to stir up its ambitious neighbour on the east coast, Argentina, and that country has recently let a contract with an American shipyard for two battleships which, according to Argentinian naval authorities, will be still more powerful Dreadnaughts than the new Brazilian ships.

For the education of young men for the army and navy the government maintains a number of schools. The Escola Militar, or military school of Rio Janeiro, is the West Point of Brazil. Here cadets are educated in military science and fitted for positions as commissioned officers. A military school is also maintained at Porto Alegre, where the children of military officers are educated at the government expense. There is also a Navy College in the same city for technical instruction in naval science. Schools for apprentices are also maintained in a number of the principal ports. The majority of those who enter these schools, both army and navy, are of mixed nationality, either negro or Indian. Instruction is given in all of the elementary studies in addition to army or naval science. The few years instruction received in those institutions by these men, who generally come from poor and ignorant homes, makes them not only better educated men but better fitted to assume the duties of citizens of a great republic.

CHAPTER XV
RELIGIOUS INFLUENCES

The Indians, whom the Portuguese found in Brazil, had not advanced in civilization as had the Incas in Peru, or the Aztecs in Mexico. They were more or less nomadic, although the different tribes kept within certain general limits as did the North American Indians. Perhaps the bounty of nature and the hot climate deadened the impulse to mental effort and exertion that leads to a higher civilization. There are evidences of the existence of the family relation and marriage customs, but polygamy was practised. Cannibalism was common too; and it is said that they not only devoured their enemies killed in war, but even ate their relatives as a special mark of favour and consideration.

The Indians generally believed in three great or chief gods. The sun was the god of the animal kingdom, the moon of the vegetable kingdom and Ruda was the god of love and reproduction. In addition to these chief gods there was a multitude of inferior deities who served various purposes. The fact that there was some idea of a future life, or a "happy hunting ground" in the beyond, is shown by the burial custom of depositing in the grave of the dead warrior the bow and arrow, and vessels in which to prepare food. It was also the custom to hang a number of friends or relatives upon the death of a chief, in order that the departed might have congenial company in the next world. The importation of negroes from Africa also brought in a great deal of superstition, and a tendency toward idolatry and fetichism, which can be traced in the religious and moral customs even to this day.

It is impossible not to admire the early missionaries of the Roman Catholic Church. They followed side by side with those adventurers and explorers who pushed their way through trackless forests and almost impassable swamps in their search for earth's treasures. It was the Jesuits who did most of the early evangelizing work in Brazil. This order was more humanely disposed toward the natives than some of the orders who accompanied the Spanish Conquistadores, for they endeavoured to protect the natives from injustice. It was in the middle of the 16th century that the members of this order began their evangelizing, work in Brazil. They plunged into regions hitherto unpenetrated by white men. They went out alone among the cannibal tribes who dwelt on these shores, and lived with them. They learned the languages, and soon were able to preach to them in their own tongues. These brave missionaries exhorted the Indians to lay aside their practice of cannibalism and polygamous marriages, and adopt the new faith. In order to appeal to their childlike natures every device and paraphernalia of pomp and procession was adopted in their services. Miraculous appearances and finds became common, so that sacred sites for the building of the religious edifices were frequently located by this means.

In order to give an unprejudiced view of the methods and purposes pursued by the early Jesuit missionaries I quote from Baron de Santa-Anna Nery,[4] himself a Catholic: "The Missionaries did not insist upon any strict theological teaching, being sure that their orthodoxy would soon be disfigured; they had but one aim in view, to render gentle and good these unhappy human beings, who gave themselves up recklessly to every impulse of their violent passions.

"The God of the Christians became for these imaginative savages the awe-inspiring *Tupan*. Satan was incarnate in the person of the terrible Anangá. Then they grasped a trinity, based upon the Catholic Trinity, and composed of the sun, the moon and Ruda, the god of love. We took part in our childhood at processions where fetich beliefs were mixed up with Christian rites. The ingenious priests who invented ceremony certainly did more than all the other preachers put together to perpetuate a semblance of the Catholic faith amongst the Indians.

"When the Indians celebrated any saint's day they erected an altar in their hut upon which they placed an image of the Saint and at its feet is placed the *Siare*. In front of the house they raise a large thatched roof. Tables are set up and everything prepared for dancing and merrymaking."

In this way were the native Indians induced to adopt at least the external forms of religion. It was not long until the majority of the aborigines became nominal adherents of the new religion. Wherever a tribe became baptized a church was erected in which to hold services, and a priest was left in charge. These priests instructed the Indians in rudimentary agriculture as well as theology, and the superiority of the educated priest over the ignorant native soon gave him a position of great vantage and influence. Power proved pleasing to the Jesuit. It was not long until the priests were really stronger than the civil authorities, and a practical theocracy sprang into existence.

They fought for the freedom of the Indian. The colonists wanted to enslave these poor natives, and make them work, willingly or unwillingly, on the plantations which they themselves were too lazy to cultivate. This was strenuously resisted by the Jesuit fathers, and by the church authorities in general, and led to many hard struggles. So when we read of the early struggles between the "Paulistas" and the Jesuits, one cannot help but sympathize with the latter, for they were championing the rights of the weak. And yet their motives do not seem to have been wholly altruistic, for they eventually endeavoured to reduce the Indians to a blind obedience to their own whims and will. Though they gave him a great measure of peace, they made him a blind servant to the will of an ambitious priesthood. The colonists continued their efforts to enslave the Indians, and in the end the Jesuits were expelled for a time from several of the states.

One of the most noted of this order was named José Anchieta, who was a native of Teneriffe, and the son of a Portuguese nobleman. It was as much due to his courage and genius as any other cause that the Jesuit influence spread as it did and became established so firmly that it has not been shaken even to this day in many sections of Brazil. He was sincere, eloquent, learned and an indefatigable worker. He went among the Indians, learned their language and acquired an almost superhuman influence among them. He became looked upon by the natives as almost divine. Water poured over his bones is said to have worked a thousand miracles, and a few drops of it are reported to have turned water into wine. Other men of power and influence there were, and a string of missions was established among all the capitancias. These reached up the Amazon to the uppermost limits of Portuguese territory, and even to the region claimed by the Spanish Jesuits, where some minor conflicts of authority ensued. The Jesuits founded a number of educational institutions in Brazil, which have exerted a great and good influence, and many of these exist even to-day. This is greatly to the credit of this remarkable order.

Bahia has always been a great centre of church influence in Brazil. There is one chapel in that city that was founded in 1582. It was built upon a spot where a miraculous image of a Virgin was said to have been discovered. And so one will find all over Brazil, as well as in Spanish-America, churches whose foundation is built upon alleged sacred spots, and many of them are now places for pilgrimages. One of these is the church of Nuestra Senhora de Peñha, which can be seen on a conspicuous height as one proceeds up the harbour of Rio de Janeiro. This church is reached by a series of three hundred and sixty-five steps. During one week in October thousands upon thousands of the natives visit this sacred shrine, and many of them climb up all of these steps on their knees as evidence of contrition, or act of penance. Everywhere church *festas* are celebrated, and many of these retain in a remarkable degree the traditions of old. In Bahia the natives celebrate one *festa* occasion by gathering together all the donkeys of the city, and elaborately decorating them with foliage and flowers.

CHURCH AT NICTHEROY.

At Pará is celebrated a *festa* which is noted in the country. The origin of the celebration is generally described as herewith given. Two hunters sought rest under the shade of a tree while returning from a hunt, and fell asleep. A strange woman appeared to one of the men in a dream, and told him to search in a thicket nearby. To his great surprise a beautiful image of the Virgin was found near the trunk of a palm tree. The two men were overjoyed at the find and presented it to the governor, who placed it in the palace chapel. On a certain day it was decided to show the image to the public, but the image had disappeared. A search disclosed it in the same thicket. A second time it was placed in the palace chapel, and a second time it found its way back to the thicket. This transpired at least twice more, although tradition differs as to the exact number of times, and then it was decided to build a chapel on that spot. This was done. Miracles have been very numerous at this shrine. Its virtues have so spread that thousands visit it, and a great procession is formed each year with the statue occupying an important position in it. Everyone joins in the procession, and the occasion is made a great event at Pará. The collection of relics in the form of wax arms and wax legs, with red spots showing where deadly wounds had been healed, and wax heads with red spots showing where sores or wounds had been cured is exceedingly ghastly. The belief of the people in these traditions is no doubt much less than in former times, and many who take part in the *festas* now probably do so principally because it is a custom hallowed by age.

It is surprising in travelling over the country to see the number of shrines and small chapels which dot the wayside and crown the summit of many hills. Some miraculous story is told about each one, and there is a shrine or relic of some kind in each one which is greatly venerated. I copy from a description given by Dr. H. C. Tucker, agent of the American Bible Society in Brazil:[5]

"In the early history of Brazil a town was often founded by setting up a Growing Stone, a Healing Cross or a Miracle-Working Image. These images are often called "Apparecido" or "Apparecida," from their "appearing" in some cave, or wild forest, stream, or on the seacoast. It is supposed that "The Lord of Matosinhos" appeared near that place from which event the brotherhood of Bom (good) Jesus of Matosinhos had its origin. The main temple or church, the seven chapels, oratorios, wooden figures seated around a table representing the Last Supper, the image of Judas and the great knife with which the pilgrims give him a dig as they pass by, the Agony in the Garden, the rough wayside cross of hardwood bearing a rude figure, dedicated to Our Lord of Matosinhos, with an inscription showing that it began to work miracles about the year 1700; the gigantic figures of the prophets, the carved work in wood and stone, the paintings of various kinds, the instruments of the Passion, the miracle-room with the large number of wax figures and hundreds of memorial tablets, representing the miracles performed by the image; the side chapels of St. Francis de Assisi, St. Francisco de Paula and others, the two pulpits, the two boxes and two open confessionals, the representation of the Trinity and the Burial of Christ, the altar tomb, covered with a board, which when removed shows a full sized effigy of Our Lord of Matosinhos, with angels kneeling around and praying, which is the grand object of the pilgrimage and where the pilgrims prostrate themselves and kiss the hand of the image with great devotion; on another side the cradle of Bethlehem, above the fine silver chandeliers:—these are some of the many curious things, in crude shape found in this church."

Sunday is a holiday, just as it is in France and Spain. The stores are usually open in the morning, but closed in the afternoon. The women go to church service in the morning, and in the afternoon all go out to the races or whatever other form of sport occurs on that day. Bull fighting was long ago abolished in Brazil, and in fact has disappeared from nearly the whole of South America. Easter Sunday is always a day for processions and solemn service in all the churches. In fact nearly a week is given over to the Easter ceremonies, when images of Christ and the Virgin and sacred pictures are carried through the streets of nearly every city and village.

The agents of the American Bible Society have traversed almost the entire republic from one end to the other in their work of distributing Bibles and Testaments. The colporteurs travel by rail, mule, steamer, canoe, or any other way that will take them to their destination, and oftentimes endure hardships almost as great as the Jesuit missionaries of old. Dr. Tucker says: "It is painfully depressing to one engaged in offering the Scriptures to hear three-fourths of them say: 'I don't know how to read.' Another obstacle is the religious superstition of the people concerning the Bible we offer them, and the belief so strongly inculcated by the priests that they have no right to read even the version accepted by the Roman Catholic Church." In one town of Minas Geraes the priest read a letter from the Bishop of Diamantina in which the people were warned against the "false Bibles" and advised that the men ought not to be allowed to stop at any place. This aroused the ignorant people to almost a fury, and cries of "Away with these heretics, kill them, kill them," were heard from numerous throats. Many armed themselves with sticks and even guns in their fanatical frenzy. No damage was done, however, for cooler counsels finally prevailed, but it is indicative of the intolerant spirit shown by the clergy—not to the work of Protestant denominations, but to the distribution of the Bible by this non-sectarian organization. Many times the books were forcibly taken from the colporteurs and burned. It also shows how different the Roman Church is in Brazil from our own land. In the United States the Roman Catholic clergy encourage education and the reading of the Scriptures to all of their flock. They maintain parochial schools at great expense in their efforts to educate the youths. They unite with other organizations in common efforts to upbuild and better the world. Some of the most severe critics have been members of that church from other countries, who have visited Brazil, and other countries of South America.

THE BEAUTIFUL CHURCH AT JUIZ DE FORA. A SHRINE ON TOP OF THE MOUNTAIN.

The Brazilian prides himself on his forbearance and generosity. So far as I could observe there is absolute freedom of worship throughout the republic. So far as official attitude goes, at least, that statement is absolutely true. It is quite possible that missionary efforts in remote districts might encounter a fanatical outburst, but, in the populated centres, missionaries are undisturbed, and they are allowed to prosecute their work free from open molestation; and everywhere that efforts have been made greater or lesser congregations are being built up.

The Methodist Episcopal Church South has the greatest number of missionaries at work in Brazil, this field having been given over to it by the Methodist Episcopal Church. It has a number of missionaries stationed in several different states, and in some places has built up fair-sized congregations. Along with its religious work it conducts a number of very excellent schools, which are doing a work that can not be measured by material standards, for education is the great need of the country. In particular, it has established schools for the education of girls, and in this work it has been very successful. Many families send their daughters to these schools in preference to the government institutions. The O Granberry

College of Juiz de Fora, which welcomes both sexes, has been mentioned elsewhere. In the same city is the Collegio Mineiro Americano, a very worthy institution with an able faculty, in which about three hundred and fifty girls receive instruction. Another very excellent girls' school is conducted at Petropolis, where they have a beautiful location up on a hill overlooking the city. Other schools are located at Piracicaba, Riberão Preto, Bello Horizonte, Rio de Janeiro and Porto Alegre.

The Presbyterian Church of the United States was one of the first denominations to begin work in Brazil. It soon gained a large number of adherents and founded that excellent institution of learning in São Paulo, Mackenzie College. Some local disagreements among the native members split the church, and one branch broke off from the parent society in the United States. This society still maintains a separate organization and has a number of congregations, but the rupture was an unfortunate occurrence. The Baptists have also begun work in several of the states. They have established schools for young boys and girls in São Paulo, Rio de Janeiro and Pernambuco. The Anglican Church has churches in several cities, but does not prosecute missionary work, as its churches are primarily for communicants of that denomination residing in the country. The Protestant Episcopal Church also has organized a few societies through missionary effort. There are quite a number of German Lutheran Churches in the three southern states where the Germans have settled, but they do not attempt any work outside of the German-speaking population. One of these churches will be found in nearly every community where there is a considerable German colony.

The Young Men's Christian Association has entered the Brazilian field in a number of places. At the present time it has associations organized in Rio de Janeiro, São Paulo, Porto Alegre and Pernambuco, with college chapters at Mackenzie and Granberry Colleges and the Military School in Porto Alegre. It is, I believe, doing a good work on the broad lines adopted by that great world-wide organization, where people of varying beliefs can unite their efforts for mutual profit, and also for the general good of the communities in which they live. There is a great field for this work, in my opinion, in this land where there is so much religious indifference among the men, who seem to leave the religious work almost entirely to the women of their families. At present these institutions are cramped in their work by lack of funds, but the secretaries, who are young Americans, are energetic in their efforts and are doing the very best they can with the resources at their command. They aid very much in the fraternizing of the native and foreign elements of the communities. It is an age of almost complete religious indifference, at least among the men of Brazil; and any movement that will rouse the people from this lethargy, either within or without the Roman school, will be beneficial to the country.

CHAPTER XVI
THE EMPIRE

The history of Brazil contains more exciting chapters, and has been the most chequered of the South American republics. Its territory has been the battleground of Spaniards, Portuguese, French, Indians and negroes. It has been successively a capitancia, a province, an empire and a republic. And yet, with all these changes and admixtures, the language, customs, religion and laws of Brazil are substantially those of Portugal. Rome gave these things as a heritage to that country, and she in turn transmitted them to her colony in the New World.

Early in the year 1500, one Pedro Alvarez Cabral, a Portuguese nobleman, sailed from Lisbon for the East Indies. Owing to some peculiar instructions that had been given to him by the King of Portugal, he sailed far west of the usual route for vessels bound to those islands. One bright morning, during Easter week, land was sighted, and his little fleet came to anchor off the coast of what is now the state of Bahia. Believing that this was only an island he named it the "Island of the True Cross," and took formal possession of it in the name of his sovereign. On Easter Sunday a landing was made, and the first mass was held. A few days later the entire fleet departed, leaving only a couple of mutinous sailors on shore.

The news of the discovery of this new land soon reached Portugal, and the Crown of that country immediately made formal claim to the territory. Expeditions were sent out by King Manuel to explore this supposed island. One of these expeditions was in charge of Amerigo Vespucci, and it was he who ascertained, after a careful examination, that this new land was a continent and not an island. Wherever the Indians were seen they were questioned about gold and silver, but, although the natives told marvellous tales of wealth, no mines were located. The only object of commercial value seemed to be the dyewood, known as brazil-wood; and, in spite of the efforts of the Church to name the country Santa Cruz, the holy cross, the name Brazil soon supplanted all other names, and has clung to the country ever since, although religious names abound in the geography of Brazil.

Scores of ships of various nationalities soon sought these shores for this precious wood, the commerce of which was exceedingly profitable. For a quarter of a century this land, teeming with fertility, remained unsettled, although explorations had been made from the mouth of the Amazon as far south as the Rio de la Plata. The resources of the country were fully appreciated, and Vespucci himself is credited with saying, that if Paradise did exist on this planet it could not be far from the Brazilian coast.

The earliest permanent settlers of Brazil were mutineers from the ships bound for India. One of these, Diego Alvarez, was put ashore at Bahia; another, John Ramelho, was left at Santos; and the third, Aleixo Garcia, found his unsought habitation still farther south. Each of these men married daughters of local chieftains, and they, and their descendants, aided greatly in the final subjugation of the country, for they allied themselves with the incomers. The first serious effort to colonize the country was begun near Pernambuco, where an attempt was made to establish a sugar plantation. This, however, was soon destroyed by some French brazil-wood hunters. An expedition, consisting of four hundred persons, was sent out under Martino Affonso de Souza a short time afterwards. After sailing along the coast he finally dropped anchor, and established the little settlement of São Vicente, near the present city of Santos, in 1532.[6] It was not long after this that the Crown divided up the whole Brazilian coast into parallel strips, each extending fifty leagues along the coast, and running inland as far as the power of Portugal extended; and these sections, called *capitancias*, were given to court favourites. The grantee was given practically sovereign powers over this territory in return for a certain tax which he was expected to pay. As a result of this arrangement a number of permanent colonies grew up on Brazilian soil. Of all the *capitancias*, that which included Pernambuco became the most prosperous because it was in the track of all the vessels from Europe, and also because it was found so well adapted to the cultivation of the sugar cane, which, at that time, was very profitable. Furthermore, little or no trouble was experienced with the Indians, who had become allies of the white men. By the middle of the sixteenth century this settlement was a flourishing one, and there were a half dozen or more communities south of it.

The *capitancia* system was not a success. Some of the grantees did not succeed; others grew to be arrogant. This aroused the jealousy of the

Portuguese government, which began to make efforts to centralize the colony, and sent out a governor-general with plenary powers and explicit directions. A capital was built in the beautiful bay of Bahia, and the success of sugar cultivation on these shores made this settlement prosperous. Negroes were imported as slaves, and Bahia continued a great distributing point of these human chattels for centuries. By the year 1585, it was estimated by a priest, that there were twenty-five thousand white people in Brazil, twelve thousand of whom were in Bahia, and eight thousand at Pernambuco. Rio de Janeiro, at that time, had a population of less than a thousand.

A TYPICAL BRAZILIAN STREET.

Other nations had been casting jealous eyes upon this Portuguese colony in the New World. A large colony of French Huguenots, seeking more congenial homes, settled at Rio de Janeiro, and formed friendly alliances with the Indians. This policy was exactly the opposite of the policy of the Portuguese settlers, who generally enslaved the aborigines wherever possible. It was several years before these French colonists were finally driven out of the country. In 1580 Brazil had become a Spanish possession through the uniting of the throne of Spain and Portugal. Spain, however, neglected Brazil, because it was not furnishing the golden wealth like Mexico, Peru and their other American colonies. The Dutch conquest about this time was far more formidable than all other opposition combined. The Dutch East India Company had been so successful in securing the greater part of the Portuguese possessions in the Pacific Ocean, that a West India Company was organized to do the same thing in Brazil. Although protected and subsidized by the Dutch government, this company was organized for private profit. A fleet of privateers, flying the flag of Holland, appeared at Bahia and captured that city; Pernambuco succumbed a few weeks later. Although there were a number of reverses the Dutch gradually extended their sovereignty until the whole of the northeastern part of Brazil was in their control. This Dutch sovereignty lasted for more than a quarter of a century, and it was not until Portugal had had its sovereignty restored, and several sanguinary battles were fought, that the Dutch West India Company relinquished its hold on these rich provinces.

During the occupancy of the northern provinces by the Dutch, development was going on in the south where Portuguese rule was undisputed. The Paulistas had by this time developed into an energetic and aggressive race. In their search for gold, and Indians whom they might enslave, they had spread their conquest over the great interior plateaus; they had rooted out all the settlements established by the Spanish Jesuits on the upper Paraná and had spread south as far as Rio Grande do Sul. Comparative commercial and governmental freedom had stimulated progress, so that by the end of the seventeenth century the population of Brazil had increased to three-quarters of a million. Many and bitter were the contests waged with the Jesuit priesthood, and the Paulistas were especially bitter in their opposition to this order. At last the Portuguese government forcibly expelled them from all Brazil. Many negroes escaped from their bondage, and fled into the interior, where they refused to recognize white supremacy, and there set up independent governments, and some of these strange republics lasted for fifty years.

It was not until the beginning of the 18th century that Rio de Janeiro became a place of importance. The discovery of gold in Minas Geraes a little while before caused a great influx of adventurers, and Rio was the only gateway to the mining territory. It soon possessed a population of several thousand and became a city of social and commercial importance.

Other communities grew and many new provinces were formed. With increasing wealth and agricultural and mineral prosperity came evidences of discontent with the body politic. The policies of the home government became narrower and narrower, as the East India possessions were lost, and they seemed determined to milk this one colony to the very last drop. The colony was neither allowed to manufacture goods, nor purchase of any country except Portugal; and this even was hampered in many ways by burdensome imposts. All business transactions were burdened with heavy fees; slaves were charged so much a head; all trades and professions were taxed at ruinous rates, and certain lines of trade were let out as monopolies to favourites. The governors interfered everywhere with the administration of justice, and bribery was rampant on all sides. Unauthorized taxes were imposed, forced loans exacted from individuals, and young men were impressed into military service.

It is little wonder that dissatisfaction grew apace. A deep repugnance spread over the land and the very name of government grew to be hated. The hostility to Portugal and aversion to everything Portuguese permeated all classes without distinction. One bright page shines out at this period of the colony's history during the administration of the Marquis of Pombal, who became prime minister of Portugal in 1750. The marquis punished bribery and incompetence without fear or favour, and for a few years the colony greatly prospered. After twenty-seven years of rule he was driven out, and the old abuses returned in even a greater degree, if such was possible. The success of the revolution in the United States about this time aroused many Brazilians to the possibility of freedom from the galling yoke. A conspiracy arose in the state of Minas Geraes, in a literary circle that existed there, but it was easily destroyed and one man, Tiradentes, was executed.

About this time an incident happened which stemmed the tide of events for a time. Napoleon was at the height of his power, and was overturning monarchies with a ruthless hand. Having conquered Spain, his armies descended upon Portugal in 1808. Fear seized the court, and Dom John, although shedding tears over his unhappy country, decided to save his own head by flight. Hence he embarked at Lisbon with all the royal family in the men-of-war, and set sail for Rio. Fifteen thousand persons, including many of the nobility and hangers-on, also embarked at the same time, together with fifty millions of property and treasure, and arrived at Rio the 8th of March, 1808. The king's first act was to issue a decree removing all the fetters on commerce, and opening up the ports to the ships of all nations. Many other decrees followed, and all restrictions upon foreigners were removed. The removal of these fetters to industrial development, and the importation of so many people, well supplied with money, inaugurated a new era for Brazil. A national bank was established, the printing press set up and many new schools founded. Scholars and artists flocked to this new capital, and the commercial nations sent their representatives. Brazil was officially designated as the Kingdom of Brazil. There were perhaps three million people in the country, of whom one-third were negro slaves, and not more than one-fourth were white. Sugar and tobacco were the great staple exports, for coffee had not at that time reached the importance that it has to-day.

The coming of the royal court to Rio was not without its disadvantages as well. Although it brought money, it also brought an extravagant government with a swarm of parasites who had bankrupted Portugal, and who now began their operations in Brazil. Money flowed freely, new offices were created to supply places for favourites, and taxes were augmented to pay these bills. Education increased, but the desire for holding office was likewise intensified. The great estates were practically abandoned, being left in the hands of slaves and subordinates. Everybody wished to live near the court, and all the young men yearned for government offices. This avidity exists even to this day, and its origin may perhaps be traced back to this period in the country's history. Politics became the popular theme—not from the theoretical standpoint, but the practical one of furnishing congenial employment at a good salary. If the salary was not large enough, then recourse was had to other sources for more revenue to keep up extravagant living.

All things have an end, and so did the royal court in Rio. Napoleon had fallen, and events of momentous importance were transpiring in Portugal. That country was jealous of the fact that the court resided in Brazil, and demanded its immediate return. A Cortes had been summoned which threatened trouble for the monarchy. The Brazilians forced King John, before his departure, to sign a decree favouring a liberal constitution such as

Spain had just adopted. This he did with, perhaps, a mental reservation, and a couple of days afterward embarked for Lisbon with a large suite.

Upon his departure King John left his son Dom Pedro, a young man just past his majority, as regent. This young man was a handsome and active youth, fond of outdoor sports and a patron of the arts. He was strong-willed, but passionate and unrestrained, and was entirely the opposite of his vacillating, weak-willed father. His manners were frank and attractive, but he loved public favour, and enjoyed being the principal dramatic figure in any crisis. His courage was unquestionable, he was prompt in decision, but he had no strong character for good. It was not long until he had the opportunity to be the central figure in truly dramatic events.

A MUD AND THATCH COTTAGE.

King John seems to have had a presentiment of coming independence for Brazil. His last words to Dom Pedro were: "I fear Brazil before long will separate herself from Portugal; if so, rather than allow the crown to fall to some adventurer, place it on thine own head." The Cortes adopted a grasping policy toward its big colony. They refused to listen to the Brazilian delegates in that body, abolished certain of the provincial courts, changed the governors, and sent garrisons to the principal cities. The attempt to transform Brazil again into the position of a province, after having been the sovereign country, aroused the whole of Brazil into indignant protest. It was looked upon as open insult. The spirit of rebellion, which had broken forth even before the departure of the court, burst out with renewed energy. The newspapers were filled with revolutionary editorials. When an order came for the return of the popular young regent the people of São Paulo, Minas Geraes and other states spoke with an almost united voice against this impolitic measure.

"How dare these deputies of Portugal deprive Brazil of her privy council, her exchequer, her board of commerce, her court of requests, and so many other institutions which promise us such future benefits? How dare they dismember Brazil into isolated parts possessing no common centre of strength and union? How dare they deprive your Royal Highness of the regency with which your august father had invested you?" In response to this and similar appeals the young prince announced that he would remain in Brazil, and thus defy the Cortes. A ministry was formed at Rio to look after the interests of the country, although independence had not been proclaimed. José Bonifacio, an energetic and able patriot, was made Prime Minister. No heed was paid to these rumblings by the Cortes, and that body continued to pass restrictive and unpopular measures. The Brazilian deputies finally withdrew in anger, and the Cortes sent armed reinforcements to Brazil. Dom Pedro issued a proclamation to the people urging resistance, and also called together a legislative assembly. The final summons of the Cortes for his return reached him near São Paulo, as he was returning from a hunt with a party of friends. Dramatically drawing his sword the regent shouted, "Independence or Death," and this cry was taken up all over the country. On the 10th of October he was solemnly crowned as the Constitutional Emperor of Brazil, and announced that he would accept the constitution to be drawn up by the assembly soon to convene. The places held by Portuguese troops soon after capitulated, and it was not long before peace had fallen over the entire new empire, although Portugal did not recognize her independence until 1825.

The mutation had been accomplished with very little opposition. The Portuguese troops were soon withdrawn, and people began to breathe more freely. Dom Pedro I, for this was his official title, had succeeded in doing what he desired; he had created a new empire with himself as the first legitimate monarch. He prided himself on establishing the first constitutional monarchy of his own free will. On every possible occasion he loudly proclaimed the beauties of the constitution and his own liberalism. His speech to the first constituent assembly was of a different tone, and was as follows: "I promise to adopt and defend the constitution which you may frame, if it should be worthy of Brazil and myself. We need a constitution that will be an insurmountable barrier against any invasion of the imperial prerogatives." This announcement served to show a change of heart in the young ruler, and caused a storm of protest from members of the assembly who were looking forward to real liberty. They desired to curtail rather than enlarge imperial privilege. The country was divided into two parties—liberal and conservative. The former party had been the leaders in the independent movement, and the Andrada brothers, members of that following, were in power. They were fiercely opposed to everything Portuguese, and were unscrupulous in dealing with personal enemies. Their policy soon ran counter to that of the Emperor, and he summarily dismissed them. He appointed a conservative ministry, headed by the Marquis of Paranaguá, and this ministry was unsatisfactory to the liberals, who had been inflamed by the dismissed Andradas.

The assembly itself became very independent and ignored the requests and recommendations of the Emperor. That royal personage himself and his Portuguese officers were attacked by both press and assembly. At last Dom Pedro arranged his troops in front of the house where the assembly met, and demanded the expulsion of the Andradas. When this was refused he enforced his demand, and immediately issued a proclamation dissolving the assembly, and deported a number of the members who were distasteful to him. A new constitution was drawn up at the inspiration of the Emperor. This instrument was promulgated as the fundamental law; but no congress was summoned, and the Emperor ruled by despotic law pure and simple. Ministers were appointed, and they soon resigned or were removed. Opposition journals sprang up and flourished. Several states at the north attempted to secede and form the "Confederation of the Equator," but this was suppressed by vigorous measures. A rebellion broke out in what is now Uruguay, and which had been claimed by Brazil. This led to war with Argentina, and a number of battles were fought between the troops of the two nations. This necessitated a large increase in the Brazilian debt, and the result was he had to acknowledge the independence of Uruguay. In 1826, by the death of his father, Dom Pedro succeeded to the throne of Portugal, but he immediately chose to remain in Brazil and abdicated in favour of his daughter Donna Maria.

A congress was finally summoned by the Emperor which met on the 3rd of May, 1826. At first this congress was timid and subservient; the second year it was less so, and by the third year it had the courage to openly defy the Emperor. He insisted that their only duty was to pass laws to increase taxes, but they endeavoured to make the ministries accountable to congress. In 1829 he dissolved this body, because of its intractability. By that act he destroyed the last remnant of his hold upon the public. The Brazilians were practically a unit against absolutism, and the native Portuguese, who upheld Dom Pedro, were in the great minority. He appointed a liberal ministry, but that was a failure. He then designated one composed exclusively of senators, but the people resented this, for senators were appointed for life by the Crown. He made a journey through some of the provinces, but his reception was unfriendly. Riots broke forth on the streets of Rio. He appointed a new ministry of reactionary tendencies, but that action failed to stem the tide. A mob composed of the best people of Rio assembled, and marched to the residence of the Emperor. The army and police were with them in sympathy, and the troops guarding his person deserted him in this hour of need. His resignation was demanded, but as firmly refused. No indignity was offered his person, but the crowd refused to disperse. At last, very early in the morning, Dom Pedro relented, and wrote out an abdication in favour of his son, a lad of only five years. "I have voluntarily abdicated in favour of my dearly beloved and esteemed son, Dom Pedro de Alcantara. I shall retire to Europe and leave a country that I have always loved and still love." These were the Emperor's words, written on the morning of the 8th of April, 1831. He immediately left Europe, where he died three years later, his life having been greatly shortened by the many excesses to which he had yielded all his life.

A GENERAL VIEW OF BAHIA.

The expulsion of Dom Pedro I left the country in an unsettled condition. Revolutionary talk was in the air and no one knew what a day might bring forth. Because of the extreme youth of the new Emperor, Congress met and selected a provisional regency consisting of three members. Trouble soon arose in Bahia, Pernambuco and Pará, and Rio seemed ready for civil war. The regency had no real ascendency and petty jealousies soon arose. In this crisis a patriot priest, Padre Diago Antonio Feijó, who had been a leader of democratic opinion, was given absolute power. He was a man of firm will and prompt execution. By his decisiveness all disorders in the capital were soon quelled. Only isolated disorders arose which were prompted by ambitious local politicians. In the provinces *pronunciamentos* were issued in high sounding language, and the populace were greatly aroused. These local disaffections sometimes gained considerable headway because of the slowness of communication. As one writer puts it, "the words 'liberty' and 'local rights,' 'constitutionalism' and 'union' were overworked in speeches and proclamations." In Pará, for instance, two hundred people were killed in one night's fighting. Ceará was in anarchy for several months and Maranhão kept up a civil war for a whole winter. Padre Feijó was an orator and a man of unswerving integrity, and soon made his influence felt, for he was respected as well. When the regency was made elective he was chosen by the electors. His one weakness was an unyielding disposition which could not harmonize the discordant elements, and he finally resigned. His successors did not do as well as the priest, who had, at least, left a record of integrity, if he had been somewhat high handed in his methods of overcoming opposition. The ten years of the regency had been about the stormiest period in the history of Brazil. Although the Emperor would not be of legal age until 1843, at the age of eighteen, a strong demand went forth for him to take charge at once. Though this was unconstitutional, no one seriously objected, and he agreed to accept the responsibility. Hence it was, in 1840, at the age of fifteen years, Dom Pedro II ascended the throne of Brazil, and administered the country for almost half a century.

The new Emperor was the antithesis of his father in tastes and disposition. Whereas the father was a sportsman, the son was a student and an omnivorous reader. The first Pedro was a man of the world, the second was the inverse. He was a conscientious monarch, and aimed to decide all questions justly. He was respectful toward religion, but the priesthood had no hold upon him. Like his father he was democratic in his manners, but was negligent in his dress and cared naught for the glitter of a court. He would rather read a favourite author than preside over a state dinner. He kept his ear to the ground, and thus generally knew the state of public opinion. The people loved him, and it was this fact alone that forefended a republic for so many years. They sometimes laughed at his eccentricities, but they respected his opinion; they had confidence in the honesty of his purpose, which was a sincere compliment to him.

Both internal and external peace generally reigned during the rule of Dom Pedro II. Rio Grande do Sul, that independent and ebullient province, remained in arms for several years, and it was not thoroughly subjected until 1845. This civil war had lasted ten years. The government aided Uruguay in her fight against the Argentine dictator, Rosas, but emerged from this fight with a number of advantages gained. The worst war in which Dom Pedro II engaged was the one waged with Paraguay, from 1865 to 1870.

This little republic was under the domination of a dictator by the name of Lopez, who, because of some fancied affront, attacked a Brazilian steamer passing up the Paraguay River. Lopez followed this up by an expedition into Matto Grosso, and easily conquered the southern portion of that province. Soon afterwards Lopez declared war against Argentina, and Uruguay was also interjected into the struggle. Thus Lopez was fighting the three republics lone-handed, each of which was more powerful than his own; but Brazil was scattered, Argentina was not homogeneous and Uruguay was disintegrated into political factions. Furthermore, Paraguay was difficult of access, especially for Brazil, and the war dragged along several years. Lopez pushed every advantage and, by the very boldness of his initiative, seemed to carry everything before him at first. Sanguinary battles were fought on Brazilian soil on several occasions. The Duke of Caxias was finally made commander in chief. This new commander was very slow in making his preparations, but the tide soon turned after he got in the field. The audacious dictator was gradually driven in; he was at last defeated and slain.

This did not supervene until nearly every man in Paraguay was slain or disabled. Brazil gained absolutely nothing. She piled up a debt of $300,000,000, and lost over fifty thousand much-needed citizens. Argentina and Uruguay profited, but Brazil, after bearing the brunt of the fighting and the lion's share of the expense, realized no substantial result.

During the entire reign of Dom Pedro II there was a ceaseless conflict going on between the liberal and conservative factions. At first the former gained the ascendency, but they failed to enact the expected reforms, so a conservative cabinet was named. The rise in the value of coffee and other profitable crops brought in an era of prosperity, which continued the conservatives in power for many years. Liberty of speech was unquestioned under this emperor, arbitrary imprisonment had ceased, property rights were respected and the administration of justice had been much meliorated. Bribery ceased to be done openly, as had been the custom before. In 1850 an epidemic of yellow fever in Rio spread consternation over the land so that even Congress adjourned in terror. Railways were inaugurated, wealth increased and luxury followed. Then came a financial crisis, and the defeat of the conservatives followed. Another boom succeeded a short period of depression, and, about the close of our own civil war, Brazil had easily made the most progress of any of the nations of South America. The mass of the people, however, were not only apathetic but ignorant; they lacked initiative and energy.

Thus it was that events drifted along with intermittent periods of prosperity and depression. The conservatives would be in power a short time, to be followed by the liberals. The Emperor retained his personal popularity, but his daughter, the Countess d'Eu, heir to the throne, was not so popular. During the Emperor's visit to the United States and Europe, in 1876, she served as regent. The general belief that she was too much under the influence of the priesthood made the people fear her possible accession to the throne, in the event of the Emperor's death or disability. There was evidently a weakening of Dom Pedro's mental powers. Because of his ill health he left the power of state with her while he went abroad in search of relief. During this regency events transpired that brought about the change from empire to republic, and the enfeebled old emperor was forced to leave the country to which he had given the best years of his life. The change could not have been long delayed, however, for Brazil was surrounded by republics, republicanism permeated the atmosphere, and the spirit of republican institutions was everywhere abroad in the land.

CHAPTER XVII
THE REPUBLIC

Three things contributed to the change of government in Brazil from empire to republic. The first of these was the natural trend toward a republican form of government, since for more than a half a century Brazil had been surrounded by republics. During that time she had been the only representative of the monarchical system on the American continent. The Emperor himself had recognized the inevitable, if one may judge from his expressions. Had Dom Pedro at that time been in good health, he would doubtless have recognized the handwriting on the wall and voluntarily abdicated. Those who were disappointed in politics, or had a fancied grievance, belonged to this republican element, as it was the only thing that promised a change. The second contributing cause was the fear of clerical domination in the event the government fell to the Princess Isabel, daughter of the second Dom Pedro and heir to the throne. That she was a devout and sincere member of the Church of Rome there was no doubt; and this made the people fear an undue influence by the priests, although she had during the regencies done no overt act. Her personality was a sharp contrast to that of the amiable Emperor, for, where he was simple and unaffected, she was autocratic and reserved. Her husband, the Conde d'Eu, was cold in demeanour, close-fisted in money matters and a foreigner—the latter being a point that the Brazilians had never been quite able to overlook. If the count had been a Portuguese nobleman the feeling toward him might possibly have been different. The third and strongest reason was the abolition of slavery, which had been urged from the throne by the crown princess the year before.

A RURAL HOME.

In order to fully understand the slavery situation it is necessary to go back a number of decades in the history of the country. At the beginning of the 19th century there were perhaps two million of negro slaves in Brazil. From about that period the movement for the abolition of slaves began to make headway. Strong and influential men arose in a number of different states and advocated the gradual eradication of this practice, by freeing all children of slave mothers after a certain age had been reached. It was not, however, until 1830, and after much agitation, that the importation of slaves was made illegal; and for many years after this there was a large clandestine infiltration of blacks. The Emperor was at heart an abolitionist and favoured the movement as much as he dared. The law of 1830 proving ineffectual, in 1854 a vigorous statute was enacted suppressing the ingress of slaves and this was strenuously enforced. At this time the slaves numbered two million five hundred thousand, nearly forty per cent. of the population. The breaking out of the Paraguayan war checked the trend of the abolition movement, but at its close, in 1870, it sprang up again more strongly than ever. In the following year the so-called Rio Branco ordinance was passed, which declared that all children of slave mothers should be free after their majority, as this service should pay for their rearing and education. Proprietors were required to register all slaves. This concession did not satisfy a large element. In a few years a powerful party arose which demanded the immediate manumission of all slaves, and this party numbered among its adherents some of the strongest men in Brazil. Slavery was abolished in the states of Amazonas and Ceará. A further bill, passed by the national assembly, declared all slaves over the age of sixty years free, on condition that they served their masters for three more years, and established a scale of low redemption prices by which the slaves could purchase their freedom. Rio de Janeiro was the centre of the abolition movement, and São Paulo of the slave-holders' strength. Many wealthy and influential slave-holders in the latter state voluntarily unshackled all their slaves for the sake of principle.

Encouraged by the state of public opinion, thousands of slaves voluntarily left the estates, and the officials generally refused aid in securing their return. So rapidly did the number of those held in bondage decrease that, by 1887, there were only seven hundred and forty-three thousand slaves in the whole empire, a little more than one-fourth of the number a quarter of a century previous. When the Congress met in May, 1888, the speech from the throne announced that "the imperial programme was absolute, immediate and uncompensated emancipation." A bill was introduced which contained the following two short articles:

I. Slavery in Brazil is declared extinct.

II. All acts to the contrary are revoked.

Within eight days the bill had passed both houses, had been signed by the princess and was the law of the country. The votes against it were hardly numerous enough to be worth the counting. By this act the strongest upholders of the monarchy were alienated.

The rejoicings were confined almost exclusively to the labouring classes, who believed this change would better their condition. Those injured, the great plantation owners, made no open demonstration, but the seeds of sedition were sown. The ambitious group of military officers, who probably saw a chance of personal aggrandizement in a change of government, realized their opportunity approaching. São Paulo was the hotbed of the disaffection, for the big coffee planters of the state felt the loss of slaves more than any other class. Furthermore that state was the home of a group of influential men who were republicans from principle. When the Emperor returned from Europe in August, 1888, an immense reception was organized for him; and that man, whose mental powers and perceptions were not so keen as formerly, failed to discern the uneasy feeling underlying the surface. And yet the plot was then well in hand for the final overthrow of monarchical conditions, as soon as a favourable opportunity presented itself.

It was not until 1884 that any avowedly republican members were elected to the national assembly, and then three were chosen, two of whom afterward filled the office of president. Benjamin Constant, a professor in the military school, in his teachings had spread republican doctrines among the younger officers of the army, and insubordination followed in certain quarters. The ministry seemed impotent against the power of the army. The princess was still disliked, and her husband, the Conde d'Eu, more so, and the Emperor was in failing health. It had been generally understood by both parties that nothing would be done during the lifetime of the Emperor. The regency of the princess had, however, become prolonged and unpopular. As the army became disaffected the conde had endeavoured to form a new Imperial Guard of Honour to protect the throne. A plan was also formulated to send the entire army away in detachments to various parts of the republic, and this was to be done on the 15th of November. It was also rumoured that the Emperor would again place the power of state in his daughter's hands. On the 14th the report became current that Constant and Marshal Deodoro da Fonseca would be arrested. The ministry did not sleep that night, as rumours had reached it that a part of the army at least would resist removal.

The republicans were busy too, and, early in the morning, a brigade of the army drew up in front of the War Department, and a peremptory demand was sent to the cabinet to surrender. Resistance was useless, for the whole army was estranged. Consequently the entire cabinet telegraphed their resignations to the Emperor at Petropolis. This reached the Emperor just as he was leaving the imperial chapel, where he had attended mass. Dom Pedro started for Rio immediately, which place he reached in the middle of the afternoon. By this time the revolutionary chiefs had met and organized a provisional government, having named themselves as ministers, with General Deodoro da Fonseca as president. A manifesto was promulgated and given to the public proclaiming a republic. The senate, which had been a life position heretofore, was declared abolished and Congress was dissolved. On the night of the 14th the city of Rio de Janeiro had indulged in a celebration, and the Emperor was an honoured guest. On the following evening he was again a guest of the city, but practically a prisoner, for a republic had been proclaimed. The Emperor was notified that he and his family would be compelled to leave within twenty-four hours, but that their lives would be protected, and ample financial provision made for them. On the night of the 16th all the royal family were placed on board a steamer bound for Lisbon. The Emperor died at Paris on the 5th of December, 1891.

The countess still resides in France with her three sons. The eldest of these, the prince imperial, arrived at Rio de Janeiro a few years ago with the intention of making a visit to the land of his birth. The federal authorities refused permission for him to land, as they feared his presence might result in a disturbance.

The opportune time for the republic had no doubt arrived, for the country at large accepted this radical change with the greatest indifference. Those who were not satisfied at least kept still and decided to await developments. Outspoken monarchists were nowhere to be found. A military dictatorship followed with many of its evils. Most of the governors of the various provinces announced their submission to the new régime, but the old officers of the monarchy were rapidly supplanted by republican sympathizers or officers of the army. This provincial government lasted for fourteen months, and effectually succeeded in making itself very unpopular. In that time a series of laws were promulgated covering almost every phase of government. The provinces were organized into states after the model of the United States of America, church and state were formally separated, civil marriage was established. Suffrage was made universal with an educational qualification only, and many judicial reforms were inaugurated. The green and yellow flag of the empire was retained although a considerable change in the design was made, and the imperial crown was eliminated from everything governmental. The republic was recognized by the United States in a little over two months, and by the other principal nations shortly afterward.

The first serious dissatisfaction arose out of delay in calling an election for a new Senate and House of Deputies. This was finally held, and the Congress met in Rio on the 15th of November, 1890. A constitution which is patterned very closely after that of the United States was adopted with few changes. One of the provisions was that the first president and vice-president should be elected by the Congress, and not by popular suffrage. Marshal Deodoro da Fonseca was chosen President, receiving eleven more than a majority, and Marshal Floriano Peixoto was selected for vice-president. The President, being a military man both by education and training, the government continued military in fact, for the constitution did not bother the new executive very much. During the provisional government the banks had been conceded the right to issue circulating notes, and the country was soon flooded with these promissory obligations. Credit was easy and a speculative boom followed. The amount of money in circulation had almost doubled in a few months, and exchange began to fall. Congress viewed this condition with alarm and passed measures restricting the issue of paper money. The President vetoed this and other bills. A law was passed nullifying the veto, and then the President forcibly dissolved the Congress. Rio was declared in a state of siege, constitutional guarantees were suspended and martial law evulgated. These measures proclaimed the President as a dictator. In Pará armed resistance arose; the State of Rio Grande do Sul openly revolted against President Deodoro, and he was unable to put it down. The revolutionists announced that they were ready to "march to Rio and depose the dictator." The navy and most of the army declared against the President and he finally resigned in favour of the vice-president, in November, 1891. The first president was an able man in many ways. He had distinguished himself in the Paraguayan war, and had held a number of responsible positions, which he filled with credit. He was too unyielding, however, and his ideas of strong and inflexible rule did not harmonize with those of others almost equally powerful.

President Floriano had his troubles from the very beginning. Those opposed to a military man for executor endeavoured to force the election of a new president, but Floriano announced his determination to serve the term for which he had been elected. He abrogated the decree of his predecessor dissolving congress, and that body at once reassembled. The relations between the executive and legislative branches of the government were smooth at first. The year 1903, however, opened with ominous murmurings, with rumours of revolutions and conspiracies. The only effect this had upon President Floriano was to make him still more severe and arbitrary. Rebellions broke out in Rio Grande do Sul again, and also in Matto Grosso. The former insurrection lasted for three years, but the latter was more quickly subdued.

In September, 1893, the entire navy under Admiral Mello, who had been Minister of Marine, revolted. The Admiral issued a *pronunciamento*, of which the following is a part, and is a fair sample of the whole: "The President of the Republic has armed Brazilians against Brazilians; and he has raised legions of so-called patriots, spreading mourning, want and desolation in every nook and corner of the Republic, for the sole purpose of gratifying his personal caprices and strengthening and perpetuating the supremacy of his tyrannical dictatorship. Promising to be the sentinel of the Treasury, the President has perjured himself and deceived the nation, opening with sacrilegious hand the public exchequer to a policy of bribery and corruption, thus abusing the authority which, in an evil hour, the revolution placed in his hands." The admiral, who had been joined by some members of Congress and other prominent civilians, threatened to bombard the city, but President Floriano acted quickly and manned, as well as strengthened, all the fortifications in the harbour. The admiral demanded the President's resignation within six hours, and that official flatly refused and defied the naval squadron.

A BRAZILIAN CRUISER.

Congress stood by the President in this crisis and voted him funds. Rio and Nictheroy were declared in a state of siege. Mello fired a few shots at the city, which did considerable damage, but did not venture to carry out his threat to bombard it. He finally escaped with the *Aquidaban* and an armed transport, the *Esperanca*, and sailed for Rio Grande do Sul to join the insurrectionists in that quarter of the republic, where a provisional government had been set up. Admiral Saldanha da Gama was left in charge of the insurgent fleet. A few months later Mello returned northward with the *Aquidaban* to Rio, but did not join the other vessels in the harbour there. Admiral da Gama attempted to establish a blockade, but the American Admiral Benham would not permit this, claiming it was an unjustifiable interruption of commerce. An attempt was made to capture the land forts and a sanguinary engagement ensued in which over eight hundred men were killed and wounded. Soon afterwards the insurgents lost several vessels which were sunk by government shells. The naval revolt finally collapsed in March, 1894, but the commander, Admiral da Gama, escaped on board a Portuguese man-of-war and joined the other admiral in the south. This guerilla war in the south lasted until 1895; and it was not until several thousand lives had been sacrificed and much property destroyed that the beef eaters of the turbulent southernmost state yielded, and a peace was once more restored which has lasted to this day. President Floriano was very severe with the rebels who were captured, and scores of them were shot. In fact, for a while, wholesale slaughter of fellow Brazilians followed. Persons who were simply suspected of being implicated in the rebellion were arrested and shot down.

The people were weary of military rule and, at the election in March, 1894, it was generally understood that a civil president should be chosen. President Floriano himself advocated this and practically selected his successor, Dr. Prudente José de Moraes Barros. A few months after his term of office expired the ex-president passed away, as had his successor, just a little while after his enforced resignation.

Republican ideas and principles made a great advance when Dr. Moraes was inaugurated as president, on the 15th of November, 1894. He was a lawyer by profession, and a native of the progressive state of São Paulo; was a little past fifty years of age, and from the earliest days of his career had been an ardent advocate of republican principles. Furthermore, the new President was opposed to the use of force in enforcing public administration. He had been a member of the provisional government of his state, and was the first governor of that state under the republic, as well as the first president of the national senate. He lived a simple life, free from all ostentation, and his straightforwardness and integrity brought to him the respect of all classes of Brazilians. Thus it was with a thorough equipment that this new civilian President met the responsible duties of his high office. The revolutionists insisted that the election was invalid, on the ground that no voting had taken place in the states of Rio Grande do Sul, Santa Catharina and Paraná, although they had no objection to the new President personally. After peace was restored the President granted amnesty to all who had borne arms against the republic.

The natural consequence of the early days of extravagance began to be felt. The national and state government seemed to have vied with each other in multiplying the number of official employees, and in spending money on public buildings and other works. To meet the deficits paper money had been issued, and now the effects of this, together with the fall in the price of coffee, were being experienced by the nation at large, and retrenchment became necessary. Enemies both in official and private circles grew up. The ruling party became split over retrenchment policies, and an attempt was made to assassinate the President in broad daylight, which, it was strongly believed, was the result of a political plot. He would have been killed, had not a brave general thrown himself in front of the President and received the fatal wound himself. The effect of this conspiracy was to increase the admiration of the people for the President, and to condemn the methods of his enemies. An insurrection arose in the state of Bahia which required federal assistance; and this was believed by many to be backed by monarchical sympathizers, for it required an army of several thousand to quell it. A *coup d'etat* which had been planned early in 1897 by the vice-president, who was in power during the temporary absence of the President to recuperate his health, and who was backed by the discontented military, was nipped in the bud by his sudden and unexpected return to the capital. The boundary line with Argentina was settled during his administration, by the arbitration of President Cleveland who determined the contention in favour of Brazil.

In this way the four years of President Moraes's term of office passed by, and Dr. Manoel Ferraz de Campos Salles, also a civilian and a lawyer, was chosen as his successor. An empty treasury, a country practically without credit, and a commercial crisis are the conditions that confronted the new President. A little later the Bank of the Republic failed, and this dragged down to ruin many commercial enterprises as well as a number of smaller banks. The President attacked these various financial problems with great energy and considerable shrewdness. The payment of interest on the public debt, which had been suspended for three years, was resumed, and the value of the money slowly began to rise. He managed by great shrewdness and tact to maintain his ascendency over the turbulent majority in Congress. The only complaints were because of the increase of taxes which were found necessary by his administration. They were able to show, however, why the money was needed and where it went. During his term another troublesome boundary question with France, over the southern limits of French Guiana, was settled. The dispute included a territory larger than Ohio, Indiana and Illinois, and was submitted to the arbitration of the Swiss government and the entire tract, except three thousand square miles, was awarded to Brazil. There were no outside wars or internal revolutions during the term of Dr. Campos Salles, and he retired at the end of his term to his home town of São Paulo, where he still lives and enjoys the confidence and regard of his fellow citizens.

The third civil President, who took office in 1902, was Dr. Francisco de Paulo Rodrigues Alves, also a Paulista, like his two immediate predecessors. He was elected peaceably, having been practically named by his predecessor. He found the condition of the government very much better than that individual had, for the finances were much improved. President Rodrigues Alves announced as his program the improvement of the sanitary conditions at Rio, and better shipping facilities. The transformation of that city, which has been elsewhere described, was the work of this administration and it remains as a monument to him. More than a thousand houses were torn down to make room for the improvements, and many millions of dollars were expended, but they were well spent. When the port works are completed, which were started by this administration, Rio will have a stone quay more than two miles in length. A special impost of two per cent. gold on all imports into that part was levied to pay for these improvements, and the government had no difficulty in floating loans to secure the money.

Another dispute over boundary, which had long been the cause of friction with Bolivia, was settled during the term of President Rodrigues Alves. This was concerning the Acre tract, which includes some of the richest rubber forests in the world. Brazil secured the land on the payment of $10,000,000, and an agreement to construct a railroad which would give Bolivia an outlet to the Amazon. It was in this territory that some American adventurers sought to set up a little independent kingdom. Several other serious boundary demarkations were likewise determined during his term of office. It was during his administration that the Pan American congress was held in Rio, which was the occasion of the visit of Secretary Root to that country, and which aided much in strengthening the friendly ties between the two countries. The consideration shown the American representative was remarkable. With the exception of a couple of little revolts which were really no more significant than strikes in our own land which sometimes require the assistance of federal troops, the administration of President Rodrigues Alves was marked by peace. He had filled many public positions and retired from office respected by all, and still lives to enjoy his honours.

In 1906 Dr. Alfonso Augusto Moreira Penna was elected President, having served as vice-president under the previous administration. He was a native of the state of Minas Geraes, and had served as president (governor, we would say) of that state. President Penna made a tour of the states before his inauguration and endeavoured to familiarize himself with their needs. His administration is too recent to be able to generalize it. All to whom I spoke, however, had only good words to say for President Penna and his aims. He desired to reform the currency by establishing a gold conversion fund. Under plans formulated by him and his advisers the government has made considerable progress along that line, and has gradually been adding to its gold reserve. His career was ended by death on the 14th of June, 1909, having served less than three years of his term, and being in the 62nd year of his age.

The duties of government fell upon the vice-president, Dr. Nilo Peçanha, who immediately entered upon the discharge of that office. President Peçanha is a native of the state of Rio de Janeiro, and was a noted lawyer in that state before his elevation to the vice-presidency. Although only thirty-nine years of age when elected to that office he had held numerous offices in his own state, including that of representative, president and national senator from that state. By reason of the constitutional inhibition he was prohibited from being his own successor to the office of president.

At the election held in March, 1910, Marshal Hermes da Fonseca was elected for the presidential term beginning the 15th of November, 1910. For the first time in the history of the republic there was an active campaign in which two candidates, Dr. Ruy Barbosa, an able lawyer, gifted orator and a civilian, opposed Marshal Hermes, on the ground that he represented the military element which had proven so unfortunate in the first few years of the republic. From the very beginning the trend was toward the Marshal, the States of São Paulo, Bahia, the home of Dr. Barbosa, and a part of Minas Geraes alone holding aloof from his banner. Nevertheless, a vigorous campaign was waged, which cannot help but be educational, for it gave the voters an opportunity they had never had before—that of choosing between two candidates. The newly-elected President was born in 1855, and began his military career at the early age of sixteen. He has successively passed through the various grades until he reached his present rank in 1906. He is considered an authority on military matters, and served as Minister of War in the last administration. There are those who fear the return of a military man to the office of chief magistrate, but the result can not be told in advance. As a citizen he stands high, and it is to be hoped that his administration will redound to the credit of Brazil.

With the single exception of the forced resignation of President Deodoro, each president has been allowed to serve his term, and his successor has been peaceably installed in the presidential chair. The semi-independence of the states has made those political organizations far too important in the Federal Union, and in many instances it has rendered local administration cumbersome and costly. During the past three presidential terms there have been no serious disturbances, and the government has made great advances in the method of administration. The elections are still arbitrary and, perhaps, in many instances unfair, but the civil presidents have been men of character, and some of them have retired from office far poorer than they went in.

A FARMER'S HOME.

CHAPTER XVIII
A LAND OF PROMISE

WANTED: ten million immigrants.

This is the cry that comes up from this great republic, for Brazil to-day possesses the greatest amount of undeveloped fertile land that is to be found in the world. The republic is still in the process of creation, but, when all the latent possibilities are uncovered, it will be a towering giant. It is in the same condition that the United States was three-quarters of a century ago. Now we have about thirty inhabitants to the square mile, while Brazil has less than six. If the workers go there, Brazil will be one of the greatest sources of food supply in the whole world long before the end of this present century. There is scarcely an article, useful either for food or raiment, that cannot profitably be raised within its borders. Great states, which are empires in themselves, are as well qualified for the abode of the white man as many of the commonwealths within Uncle Sam's borders. The heat is not such a bugaboo as many endeavour to portray it, for the Americans who live there do not complain of it at all. There are millions of untilled acres which, sooner or later, will be centres of industry and activity. This development will be difficult with individual effort, and it will be necessary for colonies to be formed with sufficient capital for aggressive work. On the Amazon, for instance, nature is too productive, too prolific, for isolated effort. It needs united and constant work and push to conquer. When once conquered, however, this very prodigality and fecundity will reward human effort, and wealth will follow. If the engineer builds a railroad, the tropical rains wash away the embankment; if the colonist turns his back on his clearing for a few months it becomes covered with a heavy growth; telegraph poles and fence posts put forth green leaves, and railroad ties have been known to sprout in the rainy season.

Will this conquest of the tropics become necessary? If the doleful predictions of Mr. J. J. Hill and others are true, the United States will soon become an importer, rather than an exporter, of food supplies, and other sources must be looked to and new virgin lands developed. We find that in spite of the rapid development of Argentina and Canada, food supplies are advancing by leaps and bounds, and every theorist is looking for a solution. Science has provided means for overcoming the sources of pollution found in the tropics, and the development can now take place under healthful conditions. Brazil is awaiting that effort. Social conditions may seem to be an obstacle; but a colony can practically establish its own social conditions, and need not be bothered to any great extent by those surrounding it. Brazil is the only country in South America where church and state have been formally separated, and this is a good indication of progress, for any form of religion may be practised without fear of disturbance.

Brazil is a very expensive country in which to live as well as travel. Nearly every article used in the house is imported, and the import duties are very high. Not only that, but the tradesmen expect an exorbitant profit in many instances. A pair of American shoes costing not to exceed $4.00 in the States will retail here for $10.00. An American who lives there came back from a visit to the States and brought back with him, among other articles, a rug and a piano. The rug cost him $20.00 in New York, and the duty amounted to $26.00. I did not learn what the piano was worth, but it cost him nearly $200.00 to get it through the customs. All goods for ladies' wear and men's furnishing are sold at correspondingly high prices.

Table supplies are very high also. Most of the grocery sundries are imported and bring good prices. Even the produce of the country is dear. Vegetables in the market sell as high as with us, while fruit, in this land which nature endowed so richly for fruit culture, is sold almost if not entirely as high as in New York. Beef is the one item that is comparatively cheap. Butter retails at 50 cents and upward a pound, eggs at 35 and 40 cents a dozen in the summer season, and all kinds of poultry for the table are correspondingly high. Café prices are expensive, except for the little cups of coffee, and it is a mystery to me how the majority of the people live, for wages are not nearly so good as in the United States. Rent is another expensive item, so that it must take every dollar the average man earns to keep up, and he cannot have anything left for a savings account.

The American drummer has been down this way with some lines of American goods. Through windows, where lovers have whispered sweet words to willing ears for centuries, there comes the busy clatter of the American sewing machine; on the coffee plantations, and even in the rubber camps, Indians, negroes and whites listen to the quavering, and ofttimes grating tones, of the American phonograph; in stores where the shopkeeper and clerk sit listlessly, as though not caring whether you buy or not, the cash is guarded by the unerring treasurer, the American cash register, and the goods are oftentimes weighed on an American computing scale; dark-eyed and dark-complexioned men pound at the keys of American typewriters, and the machine is sometimes as erring in its spelling of Portuguese as English in our own land; American farming implements may be seen rusting in the weather, just as they are neglected by our farmers in Oklahoma and Kansas; children are sometimes hauled around in little American perambulators or express wagons, and cans, which have held the products of the great oil trust, are now used to carry water from the public fountains. The Yankee medicine-man has been here, although the familiar terms of "pink pills for pale people," and other household words, are scarcely recognizable when translated into Portuguese. On the bill-boards and on walls that are centuries old, and there are many, one will see the familiar picture of a boy with a mountain codfish on his back, and the message that this medicine will lay flesh on the back of the thinnest Brazilian. American windmills turn around at the beckoning of the Atlantic breezes, and American-built engines pull the high-tariffed freight over the tortuous curves of the Brazilian railways.

Although the United States purchases almost one-third of the total exports of Brazil, yet we send to Brazil only one-tenth of the imports, and rank third in importance. This is, of course, due to the fact that it has only been within the last few years that the United States has developed into a great exporting country. It is due further to the fact that American manufacturers have not studied the markets, as have those of other countries; England and Germany in particular. British and German banks have branches in Rio, Bahia, Pernambuco, Pará, Manaos, São Paulo, Santos, and Porto Alegre, and these banks are great aids to business men from these countries. Furthermore, all of these banks make money and pay large dividends to their stockholders. At present there is no American bank in the country, or in all of South America for that matter, while Americans living and travelling there are all urging the establishment of such an institution. Personally, I believe that it would be a successful enterprise, if conducted along the lines pursued at home, for the methods of the banks working there are slow and tedious, and it requires a half hour to do what should be done in five minutes.

Another advantage of Europe has been in the matter of transportation. There are several English, German, French, Italian and Spanish lines, which run fine passenger steamers to Europe, thus giving service every few days to that continent, and affording quick transportation for freight. In addition there are many more boats, called intermediate steamers, which also carry passengers, but are slower boats and make a specialty of cargo. It is no longer necessary, however, to go to Brazil by the way of Europe, for it takes much longer and is no more comfortable. The Lamport and Holt Line maintain a bi-weekly line of steamers between New York, Bahia, Rio and Santos, and they have some excellent boats in service. The Vasari, on which I travelled, is as comfortable as any of the European boats, and has accommodation for a large number of first-class passengers. They make the trip from New York to Rio in sixteen to seventeen days, which is about the same time as the best boats from Southampton and Cherbourg, so that the passenger saves the time consumed in the transatlantic voyage. I would like to see the United States adopt the policy of encouraging a line of boats to the South American ports either by subsidy or payment for better mail service, so that there would be not only a more frequent but a quicker service. It is a mistaken economy to refuse this means of extending our commerce to the "other Americans," who naturally, and Brazil in particular, are favourably inclined, and appreciate the fraternal tie of Americanism.

Furthermore, it is necessary for American manufacturers to study the people and the market, more than has been done in the past. The Brazilians are particular what they buy, and want the best. They are not satisfied with just anything, as some seem to believe. Sometimes a change in established models might be profitable—at least it would be wise to print labels and directions in Portuguese for the convenience of the people, as well as to please them by such a compliment. Travelling representatives should be sent who not only speak the language, but understand a little bit of the Latin nature, and their methods of doing business. It is not possible to transact business in the same way that it is done at home, for there are bound to be more delays. The European salesmen understand that and cater to it. If the business is worth cultivating at all it is worth working in the proper way to accomplish results. I also believe in the establishment of American houses for the sale of American goods. At present the greater part of the American goods shipped there are sold through foreign representatives, who also handle competing goods of other countries for similar purposes. This, added to their natural preference, often leads to a secondary consideration being given to the goods of Uncle Sam. The packing system of American manufacturers has also come in for a great deal of criticism, because the goods are not packed securely. It would be an object lesson to these same manufacturers if they could see the care with which European manufacturers pack their goods. Everything is done up with the greatest care to prevent breakage and damage, while American manufacturers pack their goods in the same way that they would for a short shipment in the States; not taking into consideration the longer, harder and rougher handling to which they are likely to be subjected.

The volume of business in Brazil has reached large figures. The total imports for the year 1909, as reported by the Brazilian government, amounted to $177,731,232. This is an average importation of $10.00 for each man, woman and child in the republic. American manufacturers look with longing eyes toward China with her teeming millions. And yet the four hundred millions of Chinese used less than twice the value of imported goods as compared with the eighteen millions of Brazilians. The low wages, and consequently low purchasing power of the masses of Chinese, will, for many decades, prevent that country from becoming a great per capita importer. If the coffee situation improves there will be a wonderful increase in Brazilian imports, for many improvements are withheld in the coffee states at the present time on that account.

The exports for the same year were valued at $304,977,081. This leaves a trade balance in favour of Brazil of $127,245,849, which is a creditable showing. Some of the staple items of export are as follows: coffee, $167,375,850; rubber, $94,630,305; cacao, $9,000,000; tobacco, $9,696,685; hide, $9,097,705; maté (tea) $8,288,935; nuts, $1,121,278. The total receipts of the government for 1909 amounted to about $150,000,000, of which $93,297,952 was realized from import duties and a small balance was left in the treasury. The estimates for the present year are about $150,000,000. The total federal foreign debt is reported to be $369,087,633.38. This does not include a considerable amount of guaranteed and floating debt of the national government.

The system of raising revenue in Brazil is a perplexing and complex one as well. Some of the states have a very small land tax. It would be far better to increase this, and in that way force the breaking up of the immense estates to which some of the land is held. Instead of that, they resort to many petty little imposts to raise the necessary revenue. The principal one, of course, is an export duty on everything. Every one in the United States ought to take an interest in Brazil, for whoever drinks a cup of coffee or cocoa, eats the Brazil nuts, uses a bicycle, owns an automobile, wears rubber boots or mackintosh, has assisted in paying the running expenses of one state or another, as well as that of the national government. Therefore it is well to take an intelligent interest in what we aid in supporting.

The revenues of the national government are raised mostly by import duties. The most of these are levied by specific weight instead of *ad valorem*, so that sometimes articles which are heavy, but comparatively inexpensive, must pay a high duty. Then, in addition to regular duties, there are often special imposts levied for the construction of port works, or other public improvements. The states also have an export duty on everything sent out of the state, and sometimes even from one municipality to another. The farmer who hauls away a few bushels of beans or mandioca root must pay the export tax to the proper official, or stand a fine. All kinds of business are licensed. A merchant is sometimes obliged to pay a half dozen of these licenses, because of the different lines of goods carried. Each license permits the selling of certain specific goods. Then, in addition, there are stamp duties on all forms of commercial business, such as promissory notes, checks, drafts, receipts, etc. When you get a draft cashed a receipt is duly made out by the bank, a revenue stamp put on it and receipted by the recipient. Every article manufactured in the country bears a revenue stamp, except, as in the case with cotton goods, for instance, when so much a meter is paid to the government. Their idea is that in this way they must make up for the loss of import duties, by reason of goods being manufactured in the country. Another form of raising money is by giving out monopolies. In the city of São Paulo one man has the monopoly of the undertaking business. No one can get a burial permit until he has the consent of this man, which can only be obtained by paying him what his profit would probably be. This would depend on whether the funeral would be of the first, second or third class. The first-class funeral is very expensive, because it provides for a fine funeral car with four richly-caparisoned horses, two drivers and two footmen in elaborate livery, many carriages, and all other requirements after the same expensive fashion.

There are many lines of business that could be very profitably pursued, but it is necessary first to make a study of local conditions and requirements; and this can best be done by having a representative on the ground. The local political leaders should be consulted, so that satisfactory arrangements can be made in the way of franchise or concession for the conduct of business; and especially is this true if the business to be conducted is manufacturing. All these preliminaries should be attended to before the investment is made. These same conditions apply to many of the Latin countries, because so many of their laws are local. It is best to understand the local conditions thoroughly, and this can only be done by some one on the ground, and in touch with local conditions. After this is done the investment is safe, and in general these enterprises are encouraged in every way by the various state and municipal administrations.

Germany and England are engaged in a war for commercial supremacy in South America, and the competition is very keen. In a financial sense England practically owns Argentina, and has investments there of about $2,000,000,000. In Brazil she has perhaps $650,000,000 invested in bonds and business enterprises. It is all invested in things that have helped to develop the resources, and much of it under government guarantee. Germany has not more than half as much money invested, but her representatives have been making serious inroads on the commerce of Great Britain. At the wharves and in the warehouses the boxes and bales with German marks on them seem to predominate. In the stores German goods are driving out British manufacturers, and it is this aggressiveness that has developed the hatred of Germany one finds among Englishmen everywhere. The German caters to what he believes the Brazilian or the Argentinian wants. Some of the methods pursued by German houses, however, are reprehensible. If an American or English article proves popular it will not be long until there will be a German imitation on the market, similar in style and make, at a little cheaper price. It will probably bear an English name too, in order to carry the deception still further. Brazil is impartial in her purchases, and opens her hospitable doors to the commerce of the world. If there is any leaning or favouritism, it is, I believe, in favour of the United States. The goods sold by European merchants we can sell if the effort is made. Trade here, as in other parts of the world, is secured by the firm who can sell the best goods at the least price, in the long run, and the German will lose out in some lines, because their quality is cheap the same as their price.

The visit of Secretary Root and the battleship fleet did much to interest Brazilians in the United States; the former by the tact and the charm of his personality, the latter by the interest shown in South America. The people are still talking about both events. Money was spent lavishly. The state of São Paulo spent $250,000 on the occasion of the Root visit. Our diplomatic representatives have also been improved, and it would be difficult to find a better man for the place than our Ambassador to Brazil, Hon. Irving B. Dudley.

The Monroe Doctrine is hard for the South Americans to understand. They can not believe that it is an absolutely unselfish policy on the part of the United States, and it has undoubtedly been the cause of much political "jingoism" among their politicians. Every instance in which our State Department interferes, or takes a stand in Latin-American politics, is greedily seized upon by some element, and is frequently fostered by foreigners, who fear American influence and trade competition. The fact that it is not a clearly-defined or definitely promulgated statement leaves it open to unfair and unfavourable interpretation. Each person or country interprets it according to its own hopes or fears. The formidable strength of the United States and the recent policy of expansion has oftentimes caused the element of fear to predominate. In its best interpretation the Monroe Doctrine is rather like a big boy who makes himself a self-appointed guardian over the weaker one, which the latter does not want, and will not appreciate until he is in danger of a good whipping from a superior. It is better understood now than formerly, perhaps, but the atmosphere is still hazy when the Monroe Doctrine is mentioned. Two incidents happened while I was in South America which enabled me to observe the trend of newspaper criticism concerning this little-understood policy of the United States. It is a grave question whether it has not done more harm to possible American supremacy in South America than benefit.

"Order and Progress" is a good motto for any country. With order will come progress, and with progress order is more easily maintained. The future is painted in rosy colours by Brazilian writers and statesmen. All reasonable deductions point that way. Natural resources are there, and the greatest need is for people to develop them. It is not an El Dorado, for nothing can be accomplished without work, thought, and planning. The latent ambition of the people has been aroused, and they are looking forward into the future. The United States can take a much larger part in the development of the country than she has in the past. It is the hope of the writer that such will be the case. The American business man can do far worse than to make a little study of this resourceful republic. The people are awaiting the American merchant, manufacturer and banker; they are seeking the American scientist, educator and expert in all lines; and they will welcome the American traveller who is searching for a good opportunity of investment.

www.ingramcontent.com/pod-product-compliance
Lightning Source LLC
Chambersburg PA
CBHW081616100526
44590CB00021B/3464